SPLIT-LEVEL
Dykes To Watch Out For

Other books by the author:

The Indelible Alison Bechdel: Confessions, Comix, and Miscellaneous Dykes To Watch Out For

Hot, Throbbing Dykes To Watch Out For

Unnatural Dykes To Watch Out For

Spawn Of Dykes To Watch Out For

Dykes To Watch Out For: The Sequel

New, Improved! Dykes To Watch Out For

More Dykes To Watch Out For

Dykes To Watch Out For

SPLIT-LEVEL
Dykes To Watch Out For

by Alison Bechdel

Firebrand
Books
Ithaca, New York

Alison Bechdel's cartoons appear regularly in over sixty publications internationally.

Book and cover design by Alison Bechdel and Debra Engstrom

Printed in Canada

10 9 8 7 6 5 4 3 2 1

Library of Congress Cataloging-in-Publication Data

Bechdel, Alison
    Split-level dykes to watch out for / by Alison Bechdel.
    p.   cm.
    ISBN 1-56341-102-4 (pbk. : alk. paper). — ISBN 1-56341-103-2 (cloth : alk. paper)
    1. Lesbians—United States—Comic books, strips, etc.
2. Lesbianism—United States—Comic books, strips, etc.   3. American wit and humor, Pictorial.   I. Title.
HQ75.6.U5B425   1998
306.76'63'0207—dc21   98-44382
                                                      CIP

for Amy Rubin

For their patient and thoughtful help with crazed, last-minute research questions, I'm grateful to Susie Day, Deb Lashman, Ben Lashman-Van Buren, Jackie Marino, Manny Neuzil, Melinda Scott, Barbara Smith, Jane Van Buren, and Pat Winer. I'm indebted to Bonnie Morris, Esther Rothblum, Linnea Stenson, and Kerry Walk for the generous career advice they've provided for my academic characters. Thanks to Paula Myrick, Amey Radcliffe, Ann Reading, Steph Salmon, and the Copy Goddess, for their sundry technical assistance. Thanks to Sarah Van Arsdale, Morgan Shore, and Lynette Reep, for modeling and moral support. To Helen Bechdel, for all the late-night grammar and reference aid. To Amy Rubin, for her lavish editorial help, and for all the ideas in this book that are really hers. And to Nancy Bereano of Firebrand Books, my publishing heroine, for keeping the press rolling.

When we last dropped in, things were looking uncharacteristically copacetic for our bevy of beguiling babes.

Housemates Lois, Sparrow, and Ginger are navigating the challenging interpersonal dynamics of collective living with skill and magnanimity.

In a final manic binge, **GINGER** completes the dissertation she's been writing for the past ten years.

Sparrow is assiduously pursuing her directorship of the women's shelter.

AFTER BEING DUMPED BY HER LATEST FLING, THE LIBIDO-INHIBITED **LOIS** IN TURN DUMPS HER PROZAC.

CLARICE, TIRELESS ATTORNEY FOR THE ENVIRONMENTAL JUSTICE FUND, **TONI**, PART-TIME ACCOUNTANT, AND **RAFFI**, FULL-TIME THREE YEAR-OLD, SUCCESSFULLY PETITION THE STATE TO BECOME A LEGAL NUCLEAR FAMILY.

...AND SINCE YOUR SON SEEMS PERFECTLY NORMAL AND HEALTHY, I CAN FIND NO LEGITIMATE REASON TO DENY THIS ADOPTION.

TOO GOOD TO BE LEGAL

TONI'S PAL **CARLOS** HELPS OUT WITH CHILD-CARE IN HIS COPIOUS SPARE TIME.

IT'S THE SAME WITH DANIEL. JUST BECAUSE I'M BETWEEN JOBS, HE THINKS I HAVE TIME TO STAND AROUND IRONING HIS DRAWERS. OH, I BROUGHT YOU THE TAPE OF YESTERDAY'S "ALL MY CHILDREN."

...AN' DEN HE CUTS HIS HAIR AND MAKES **SUCH** A MESS.

AT MADWIMMIN BOOKS, **JEZANNA** INTRODUCES A BREATH OF FRESH AIR.

...AND IN HERE IS MY DILIGENT STAFF. HOPELESS WORKAHOLICS, AS YOU CAN SEE. EVERYONE, MEET OUR NEW INTERN, ANJALI.

OH, WOW. I AM TRIPPING **OUT** THAT I ACTUALLY GET TO WORK HERE!

HARD CORE

©1997 BY ALISON BECHDEL

From East Grand Forks to Key West, queer America huddles 'round its home entertainment centers for a telehistoric moment of collective catharsis.

...AND WHAT WAS **HIS** NAME?

SUSAN.

264

Ha Har Hyuk!

...I GUESS WHAT I'M TRYING TO SAY IS, I GOT THE JOKE ABOUT THE TOASTER OVEN.

SNIFF sniff

...I WANT A HOUSE WITH A PICKET FENCE, YOU KNOW, A DOG, A CAT, SUNDAY BARBECUES, SOMEONE TO LOVE...

AARGH!

YES, I'M... I'M GAY.

DON'T YOU SEE WHAT'S HAPPENING HERE? THEY'RE TRYING TO **NEUTRALIZE** US! THEY FEED US SOME PHONY SITCOM ABOUT OUR LIVES SO WE'LL STAY HOME AND **WATCH** IT, INSTEAD OF GOING OUT AND MAKING OUR **OWN** SUBVERSIVE CULTURE!

WELL, JERRY FALWELL SEEMS TO FIND THIS SHOW PRETTY DAMN SUBVERSIVE. BESIDES, IT'S **NOT** PHONY. SHE'S A REAL LIVE LESBO!

THAT'S THE WORST PART! TRY TO CHANGE ANYTHING IN THIS COUNTRY AND YOU END UP GETTING **PACKAGED** AND **SOLD BACK** TO YOURSELF! PLUS NOW EVERY SHMOE ON THE STREET'S GONNA THINK THEY KNOW WHAT MY LIFE IS LIKE!

11

let the lover beware

© 1997 BY ALISON BECHDEL

Mo'S HAVING A COFFEE BREAK WITH EVERY-BODY'S FAVORITE CONFIDANTE.

(265)

I CAN'T EXPLAIN IT! SHE'S SO IRRITATING ...YET SO SEXY! I CAN'T STOP THINKING ABOUT HER!

GIVE ME THE PARTIC-ULARS.

IT'S THE BEST SEX I EVER HAD!

NOT NECESSARILY A GLOWING TESTIMONIAL IN YOUR CASE. SO, HOW'D YOU LIKE THE "CYBORGASM?"

WHAT?

YOU KNOW! THAT DILDO SYDNEY BOUGHT AT THE STORE LAST WEEK. THE WEIRD, RIDGY ONE. I HAVEN'T TRIED IT YET.

I... YOU... HOW...

I'LL TAKE THAT AS A POSITIVE REVIEW. I'M ASSUMING SHE WORE IT. OR DID YOU STRAP 'ER ON TOO?

LOIS! THERE'S MORE TO SEX THAN MERE TECHNIQUE. I'M TRYING TO TELL YOU I REALLY LIKE THIS WOMAN! A LOT!

WHOA, BIG FELLA! THERE'S NOTHING WRONG WITH JUST HAVING A GOOD TIME. I WOULDN'T RUSH INTO ANYTHING WITH SOME-ONE LIKE SYDNEY.

WHADDAYA MEAN, SOMEONE LIKE SYDNEY? JUST WHAT EXACTLY IS SYDNEY LIKE?

ME.

12

Meanwhile, over at the university...

HEY, SYDNEY. YOU READY TO LEAVE?

YEAH. CAN YOU HELP ME CARRY THIS STUFF TO THE CAR?

KNOK

SYDNEY

AH! YOU'VE FINALLY REALIZED WHAT A **CROCK** QUEER STUDIES IS, AND YOU'RE DONATING ALL THESE BOOKS TO THE CONCERNED WOMEN FOR AMERICA RUMMAGE SALE.

SADLY, NO. THIS IS ABOUT HALF THE READING I NEED TO DO THIS SUMMER FOR MY BOOK. THE PRESSURE'S REALLY ON FOR ME TO PUBLISH.

SYDNEY KRUKOWSKI

QUE(E)RYING EVERYTHING

HOW NICE TO KNOW THIS DELIGHTFUL STRESS WON'T END AFTER I DEFEND MY DISSERTATION NEXT WEEK.

WELL, LOOK ON THE BRIGHT SIDE. THERE'S SUCH A GLUT OF PH.D.S YOU'LL PROBABLY NEVER FIND A JOB.

SYDNEY KRUKOWSKI

ZIP!

AT LEAST I'D HAVE A LIFE AGAIN. HAVE YOU TOLD MO YOU'RE GONNA BE SPENDING THE SUMMER WRITING THIS BOOK?

NO. WHY? DOES SLEEPING WITH SOMEONE A FEW TIMES MEAN I SHOULD CONSULT HER ABOUT MY CAREER?

CLIK

Dole BANANAS FOR YOU

HEY, GIRLFRIEND. DON'T PRETEND THIS IS SOME KIND OF CASUAL SEX THING. I KNOW MO BETTER THAN THAT.

LOOK, THERE'S NOTHING WRONG WITH JUST HAVING A GOOD TIME.

EXIT

MMM. I KNOW A LOT OF PEOPLE WHO'D HATE TO SEE MO GET HURT, IS ALL. SAY, I HOPE YOU SAVE YOUR MANUSCRIPT ON MULTIPLE DISKS. IT'S SCARY HOW VULNERABLE ALL THOSE YEARS OF RESEARCH ARE, ISN'T IT?

GULP!

Dole PESTICIDES FOR THE THIRD WORLD

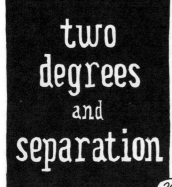

two degrees and separation

©1997 BY ALISON BECHDEL

266

HEY, SPARROW. AM I INTERRUPTING A PRIVATE MOMENT WITH THOSE PEACHES?

OH, HI, MO. HEY, I LEFT A MESSAGE FOR YOU. I KNOW IT'S TOTALLY LAST MINUTE, BUT WE'RE HAVING A LITTLE DINNER TONIGHT TO CELEBRATE GINGER GETTING HER PH.D. CAN YOU COME?

JEEZ, I'D LOVE TO, BUT SYDNEY'S COMING OVER. I'M MAKING CURRIED ARTICHOKE AND MUNG BEAN GUMBO. IT'S SUPPOSED TO BE SOME KINDA **APHRODISIAC.** NOT THAT WE NEED ANY HELP.

OH, OKAY. MAYBE SOME OTHER TIME.

YEAH. ARE YOU OKAY? YOU LOOK KINDA TIRED.

DRIED STUFF on sale

OH. UH... THINGS ARE REALLY HARD AT THE SHELTER. WE JUST LOST HALF OUR FEDERAL FUNDING, AND WE'VE GOT MORE WOMEN THAN EVER WHO NEED HELP.

SPARROW, IF YOU'RE GONNA STAND HERE YAKKING, GIVE ME THE LIST.

UH... HI, JUNE.

THAT'S AWFUL! WHAT'RE YOU GONNA DO?

WELL, I HAVE THIS NEW PLAN. WHEN REPUBLICAN POLITICIANS FINISH A TERM IN OFFICE, THEY HAVE TO SPEND THE REST OF THEIR CAREERS PROVIDING DIRECT SOCIAL SERVICES. SORT OF AN INCENTIVE PROGRAM.

ACTUALLY, WHY STOP WITH THE REPUBLICANS? **CLINTON'S** THE ONE WHO JUST SIGNED THAT SPINELESS BUDGET AGREEMENT, SLASHING DOMESTIC SPENDING SO ALL THE OPPRESSED **KAJILLIONAIRES** CAN GET A CAPITAL GAINS TAX BREAK!

THREE SEVENTY-NINE FOR A LOAF OF BREAD! I TOLD YOU WE SHOULD'VE GONE TO SHOP 'N DROP!

THUNK!

AND THE THING IS, IT'S A **VICIOUS CIRCLE!** THE MORE MONEY BIG CORPORATIONS MAKE, THE MORE LEVERAGE THEY HAVE TO GET BUSINESS-FRIENDLY LAWS PASSED, LIKE "WORKFARE" BILLS THAT SUPPLY THEM WITH DIRT-CHEAP LABOR. **THEY'RE** RAKING IN MORE THAN EVER WHILE **OUR** TAXES GO UP AND REAL WAGES GO DOWN.

SPARROW, TAKE IT EASY! THOSE ARE ORGANIC!

SPLORT!

Later...

FINE. MOVE AWAY IF YOU HAVE TO. BUT FOR **BUSINESS SCHOOL?**

GOD! WILL YOU STOP ACTING LIKE I'VE MADE A PACT WITH THE DEVIL? GETTING AN M.B.A. IS NOT A CRIME!

@ AT THE UNIVERSITY...

SYDNEY! EVERYONE FINALLY SIGNED OFF ON THIS THING! COME FILE IT WITH ME AND THEN WE'LL GO TO MY PLACE. SPARROW'S MAKING A CELEBRATION DINNER.

SYDNEY OWSKI

GREAT! MO AND I WERE GONNA DO SOMETHING, BUT I'LL CALL AND GET A RAIN CHECK.

RING!

THE Herbivores companion

15

IT'S THE EVENT O' THE SEASON!

BLUE PARTY

© 1997 BY ALISON BECHDEL

267

YOU'RE GOING TO GINGER'S PARTY? ...YEAH, I **KNOW** IT'S A BIG DEAL SHE FINALLY GOT HER DOCTORATE. I MEAN, I WAS INVITED TOO, BUT I TOLD SPARROW WE ALREADY HAD PLANS. I'M MAKING MY SPECIAL MUNG BEAN GUMBO!

WELL, WHY DON'T GINGER AND I PICK YOU UP? THAT WAY WE'LL SEE EACH OTHER **AND** GO TO THE PARTY! KILL TWO BIRDS WITH ONE STONE.

SHH!

SUCH A ROMANTIC.

@MEANWHILE...

WHAT AM **I** SUPPOSED TO DO WHILE YOU'RE OFF IN BOSTON AT BUSINESS SCHOOL? SIT HOME KNITTING YOU POWER TIES?

WELL... I DUNNO. MAYBE WE SHOULD TAKE A BREAK, SEE OTHER PEOPLE FOR A WHILE.

CHOP CHOP!

WHAT?

IT'S A TWO YEAR PROGRAM. I DON'T EXPECT YOU TO JUST WAIT AROUND.

URF.

CLIK

HI! I PICKED UP THE CAKE. NEED HELP WITH DINNER?

SOB!

SWEETIE, I'M JUST THINKING OF YOU!

dirty movies

One summer's morn...

OH, GREAT! "WATERMELON WOMAN" IS AT THE THALIA! WANNA GO TONIGHT?

I CAN'T...I'VE GOTTA WORK ON MY BOOK. IN FACT, I WON'T BE ABLE TO SEE YOU ALL WEEKEND.

CHERYL DUNYE'S N.E.A. FUNDED FILM IS "FLOTSAM FLOATING DOWN A SEWER." SEZ JESSE HELMS

268

POST-MORTEM POSTU-LATIONS

GOD, SYDNEY! WHAT AM I, A YO-YO? EVERY TIME WE GET CLOSE, YOU PUSH ME AWAY AGAIN!

I'M NOT PUSHING YOU AWAY! I JUST HAVE WORK TO DO! WHY CAN'T YOU UNDERSTAND THAT?

"NOW BENJI, THERE'S A FILM!" SENATOR CONTINUES

POSTNASAL PARADIGMS

OH, I UNDERSTAND! YOU ONLY SEE ME WHEN YOU WANNA **BUMP** "LIBIDINAL SURFACES" INSTEAD OF **THEORIZE** ABOUT THEM!

MMM...I **LIKE** IT WHEN YOU USE POSTMODERN JARGON! COME BACK TO BED...

Down at the bookstore...

CAN I BUM A CIGARETTE, ANJI?

SINCE WHEN DO YOU SMOKE?

SINCE I WANT AN EXCUSE TO LOITER OUT HERE INSTEAD OF WORKING.

HEY! HAVE YOU SEEN THAT MOVIE "ALL OVER ME?"

Panel 1: No. I was gonna go this weekend.

Lois, you hafta take me! Just because it has two girls kissing, they rated it 'R.' If I go with someone older, I can pass for eighteen.

Panel 2: Sure. Heck, next to an old hag like me -KOFF-. You'll look middle-aged.

D'you think? Maybe to be safe, I'll borrow my mom's K.D. Lang T-shirt.

Panel 3: I've sent out thirty-five resumés and gotten zero calls. No one wants to hire an accountant who's been out of the job market for four years.

These listings are either for night janitors, or people with "solid experience in RS232/485." What am I gonna do?

Panel 4: You really should take a basic computer class.

I'd rather take in an air-conditioned matinée. Let's go see **Hercules**.

Weekend

Panel 5: Absolutely not. I'm trying to restrict his Disney intake.

You have to go, querida, or people will think you're a Southern Baptist!

Hewkuwees!

Fundamentalists boycott Disney for gay-friendly policies

Panel 6: Okay, okay! I'll come to the movies with you! Now say it! Please!

Oh, baby. Let me privilege lesbian positionality by destabilizing your bodily metanarrative.

McOnomics

269

OH MY GOD! THIS IS SO 1984!

The Daily Newspeak
UNEMPLOYMENT GOOD
HIGH WAGES BAD

NOW CORPORATIONS ARE DETERMINING WHAT **LANGUAGE** WE CAN USE! THE OXFORD ENGLISH DICTIONARY JUST DECIDED NOT TO INCLUDE AN ENTRY FOR THE WORD "McJOB."

HEY! BE CAREFUL. I HAVEN'T READ **MARK TRAIL** YET.

THEY'RE INTIMIDATED BECAUSE McDONALD'S JUST SPENT $15 MILLION TO WIN A LIBEL SUIT AGAINST TWO PENNILESS BRITISH ACTIVISTS WHO DARED TO SAY THAT A **BIG MAC** ISN'T THE **HEALTHIEST** THING IN THE WORLD YOU CAN EAT!

BUT EVERYONE KNOWS FAST FOOD TOTALLY ROTS! HOW CAN THAT BE LIBEL?

The Distress

TOUCHING, ISN'T IT? WAS I EVER THIS INNOCENT?

ANJALI, LET ME TELL YOU A THING OR TWO ABOUT HOW BIG BUSINESS WORKS. FIRST OF ALL, WITH ENOUGH JACK, YOU CAN PROVE **LARD** CURES **COLON** CANCER.

DUH! I THINK I UNDERSTAND THAT GLOBAL CAPITALISM IS COLONIZING HUMANITY AS WELL AS THE PLANET IN AN EVER-EXPANDING AND INCREASINGLY **BRUTAL** QUEST TO FEED A HANDFUL OF BLOATED MULTINATIONALS, MO!

BUT IF YOU'RE FEELING MENTOR-ISH, EXPLAIN **THIS** TO ME. GIVEN THAT MEGACORPORATIONS ARE TURNING OUR COMMUNITIES INTO A **SOULLESS EXPANSE** OF **CHAIN STORES**, AND SIPHONING OFF LOCAL WEALTH TO DISTANT CEOs WHO EARN **140 TIMES** WHAT THEIR WORKERS DO, WHY DO AMERICANS FLOCK TO PLACES LIKE McDONALD'S AND WAL-MART INSTEAD OF RISING IN COLLECTIVE **REVOLT** AGAINST THE UNJUST ECONOMIC ORDER?

UH...

HEY.

SLEATER KINNEY

MAN, YOU WON'T BELIEVE WHAT I JUST HEARD. A **BOUNDERS BOOKS AND MUSIC** STORE MIGHT MOVE IN DOWN THE BLOCK. JEZANNA WILL FLIP!

AS IF THE **BUNNS AND NOODLE** OUT AT THE MALL WASN'T ENOUGH. NOW WE'LL HAVE **TWO** SUPER-STORE CHAINS TO COMPETE WITH. ANYONE WANT SOME FRIES?

UM...NO THANKS.

IT'S ALL THAT SATURATED FAT. CLOGS THE NEURAL TRANS-MITTERS AND IMPAIRS THE BRAIN'S ABILITY TO MAKE CONNECTIONS.

OH. THAT'S WHAT I THOUGHT.

SCHLRRP!

the mythology of everyday life

©1997 BY ALISON BECHDEL

270

OUR HEROINE RETURNS HOME FROM HER LABORS.

YOU LOOK LIKE YOU'VE BEEN PARBOILED, SWEETHEART.

HI, MEEMA.

UNH. OUR AIR CONDITIONER DIED, AND THE ONLY THING I HAD TIME TO EAT ALL DAY WAS A SNO-CONE.

OH, CLARICE. I HAVEN'T EVEN THOUGHT ABOUT DINNER YET! WE JUST GOT BACK FROM THE MOVIES.

HERCULES. IN DIGITAL STEREO AIR CONDITIONING.

HOW NICE FOR YOU. IN CASE YOU'RE WONDERING WHAT **I** DID TODAY, I WON AN INJUNCTION AGAINST A NITRIC ACID PLANT, THEN I FAILED TO PREVENT 300 ACRES OF WETLANDS FROM BEING TURNED INTO A **LANDFILL**, THEN MY CASE AGAINST A PESTICIDE COMPANY GOT **DISMISSED** ON PROCEDURAL GROUNDS.

MEEMA! IN DA MOVIE, HEWKUWEES, HE, HE, HE CUT OFF DA MONSTOW'S HEAD AN' DEN IT GWEW MOW HEADS!

IT GREW MORE HEADS? HUH. THINGS HAVEN'T CHANGED MUCH IN THREE MILLENNIA.

OOPS.

HEY, THAT BEER LOOKS GOOD.

SWEETIE, THAT WAS THE LAST ONE. HOW ABOUT SOME NICE, COLD APPLE JUICE?

R&R

©1997 BY ALISON BECHDEL

271

OUR PREOCCUPIED PALS HAVE PACKED UP ALL THEIR CARES AND WOES AND BROUGHT THEM TO THE BEACH.

MO! YOU'RE GETTING SAND IN MY KEYBOARD!

WHY'D YOU BOTHER COMING IF ALL YOU'RE GOING TO DO IS WORK?

FLAP

OPERATIONAL BUDGET

MO BRIBED ME WITH SEXUAL FAVORS.

SYDNEY!

WELL, YOU DID.

Y'KNOW, YOU TWO ARE REALLY GETTING INSUFFERABLE.

YEAH. HAVE A LITTLE RESPECT FOR THE GRIEVING.

SPARROW, JUNE ISN'T DEAD. YOU DUMPED HER.

OH, SO I'M NOT SUPPOSED TO HAVE ANY FEELINGS ABOUT IT?

MAMA?!

YOU'D BEST GET YOURSELF ON A PLANE, GIRL. I'M NOT LONG FOR THIS WORLD.

MAMA! WHAT'S GOING ON? DID SOMETHING HAPPEN? ARE YOU STILL AT HOME?

HI, BABY. IT'S ME. SHE JUST NODDED OFF. THE PAIN WAS REALLY BAD THIS MORNING AND SHE NEEDED A LOT MORE MORPHINE.... HOW CLOSE IS SHE? I CAN'T PREDICT THAT, HON. BUT SHE WON'T TOUCH YOUR COUSIN ETTA'S POT ROAST, AND SHE REALLY WANTS TO SEE YOU.

MEANWHILE...

WHAT AM I WEARING? YOU MEAN RIGHT NOW? A STRIPED SHIRT AND A PAIR OF JEANS. WHY?

MO!

BEST LESBIAN EROTICA OF AUG. 1997

CLEAVAGE PRESS

GOTTA GO, SYDNEY!

I'M CATCHING A 3:30 FLIGHT. MY MOTHER'S WORSE. I'LL CALL EVERY DAY TO CHECK IN. TRY NOT TO BANKRUPT US, OKAY?

UH...RIGHT. HEY, JEZ...I HOPE SHE'LL BE...YOU KNOW, OKAY.

UM... TAKE CARE.

Change to Spare

© 1997 BY ALISON BECHDEL

YES, I'M SURE! I NEED A CHANGE! MY LIFE IS TOTALLY **STALLED.**

I DUNNO IF THIS WILL CHANGE YOUR LIFE. BUT I WISH YOU AND JUNE HAD BROKEN UP YEARS AGO IF THAT'S WHAT IT TOOK TO MAKE YOU CHANGE THIS WASHED-UP 'DO.

The Chop Shop

2·73

OH, REALLY. SPEAKING OF WASHED-UP, I HEAR YOU'RE NOT HAVING MUCH LUCK SELLING YOUR SECOND BOOK.

HEY, I CAN'T HELP IT IF ALL PUBLISHERS WANT IS "BILLY GRAHAM'S FAVORITE LOW-FAT CHICKEN SOUP FOR THE SPIRIT RECIPES."

VITA SINE LITTERIS MORS EST

GEL

LATER...

GRRR!

DIGGER, **RELAX!** IT'S ONLY ME.

...AND CYNTHIA COOPER GETS INSIDE FOR TWO!

GO, COOP!

SNIFF SNIFF

GINGER! WHAT'S BURNING?

AAA!

...CHARLOTTE LEADS HOUSTON 54-39. YOU'RE WATCHING THE WNBA ON NBC.

28

29

all for one

© 1997 BY ALISON BECHDEL

The first prospective buyers have just finished touring our hapless housemates' home.

274

I don't know... it's not the greatest neighborhood.

But the price is right. And once we fixed the place up, it'd really improve the whole block.

Thanks, hon. We'll try and give you more notice next time.

You do that.

I bet the wife hyphenates their last names and the husband just uses his own.

Nice touch, Lois, the dildos all tucked under your covers like they were going to sleep. I'd swear Brad and Janet blanched, if they weren't so colorless to begin with.

I can't live like this! Strangers traipsing through the house, not knowing where we'll be in two months... we've gotta DO something!

Maybe another landlord'll buy the place and we won't have to do anything.

More likely, Ms. Minivan-Hyphen will be moving in with her Laura Ashley toilet paper.

31

handling it

© 1997 BY ALISON BECHDEL

IT'S BEEN A LONG DAY AT THE HELM FOR OUR HEROINE...

MO, REMEMBER, I'LL BE OUT TOMORROW AND FRIDAY FOR ROSH HASHANAH.

SKREE

275

MADWIMMIN BOOKS

Closed

OH, RIGHT. DAMN! I'LL HAVE TO CANCEL MY CHIROPRACTOR APPOINTMENT.

DON'T GIVE ME ANY GRIEF. YOU HAD PLENTY OF WARNING. NOT THAT YOU SHOULD NEED IT.

I KNOW, I KNOW. IT'S FINE. HAPPY NEW YEAR.

THANKS.

SHANAH TOVAH, BABE.

Y'KNOW, THERE'S NOT MUCH POINT IN GOING OUTSIDE TO SMOKE IF YOU'RE JUST GONNA STAND IN FRONT OF THE DOOR.

WHY ARE YOU SMOKING WITH HER, ANYWAY? YOU SHOULD BE SETTING AN EXAMPLE!

AND YOU! FOR ALL YOUR SOPHISTICATED POLITICAL ANALYSIS, YOU'RE PLAYING RIGHT INTO THE TOBACCO INDUSTRY'S HANDS! THE YOUNGER THEY HOOK YOU, THE BIGGER THEIR PROFITS!

Lilith Fair

spaced out

© 1997 BY ALISON BECHDEL 276

Panel 1: SO THE POSSIBILITY OF THE CASSINI PROBE HURTLING BACK INTO EARTH'S ATMOSPHERE WITH 70 POUNDS OF DEADLY PLUTONIUM ON BOARD DOESN'T GIVE YOU EVEN A SLIGHT QUALM?

NAH.

Panel 2: HOW DOES SOMEONE WHO PRIDES HERSELF ON HER CRITICAL THINKING SWALLOW NASA'S PRO-NUCLEAR PROPAGANDA SO BLITHELY?

I EXPECT IT'S SIMILAR TO THE WAY YOU SWALLOW THE LEFT'S ANTI-SCIENCE PROPAGANDA WITH SUCH CAREFREE >SNIFF< ABANDON.

Panel 3: OH, SO I SHOULD TRUST A BUNCH OF GOVERNMENT "DUCK AND COVER" FLACKS OVER THOUSANDS OF SELFLESS PEACE ACTIVISTS.

MO, I CAN'T ARGUE WITH YOUR KNEEJERK >SNIFF< OVERSIMPLIFICATIONS. DAMN!

Panel 4: YOUR ALLERGIES?

YEAH, AND I DON'T HAVE MY PILLS. I'M GONNA HAVE TO LEAVE BEFORE IT GETS WORSE.

HONK

Panel 5: HOW COME YOU WEREN'T ALLERGIC TO MY CATS WHEN WE FIRST STARTED GOING OUT?

ENDORPHINS OFTEN OVERRIDE ALLERGIC REACTIONS. I READ A PAPER ON IT ONCE. WHERE'S MY SCARF?

ZIP

OVER AT CLARICE & TONI'S...

HNG!

ARR!

Clik

CRUNCH!

THIS PLACE IS DRIVING ME **NUTS!** THE BEDROOM CLOSET'S SO PACKED, ALL MY SUITS ARE CRUSHED. AND I RIPPED THIS THING TRYING TO GET THE DOOR SHUT.

STINKY!

GREAT. THAT WAS HIS FAVORITE BEANIE BABY.

crunch

WAIL!

ALL RIGHT, ALL RIGHT. I'LL LOOK AT IT.

REAL ESTATE EXTRA

MEANWHILE...

THE REALTOR'S BRINGING SOME PEOPLE OVER AT SEVEN. I'M GOING BACK TO SCHOOL AND GRADE PAPERS.

I SHOULD GO TO THE GYM ANYWAY.

AND I'VE GOT A... I MEAN, I'M HAVING DINNER WITH SOME-ONE.

IS "SOME-ONE" PICKING YOU UP, OR CAN I GIVE YOU A RIDE "SOME-WHERE?"

WHAT'S THE BIG MYSTERY? IS SHE IN A RELA-TIONSHIP? MARRIED? HIGH PROFILE AND IN THE CLOSET?

DOES THE YWCA STILL RENT ROOMS? MAYBE I'LL CHECK IN THERE TILL I CAN FIND MY OWN SPACE.

suburban subversion

©1997 BY ALISON BECHDEL

disclosure

Mo's HAVING A LITTLE HOLIDAY CHEER WITH SYDNEY'S FATHER AND STEP-MOTHER.

(278)

I DON'T KNOW WHY HARVARD TURNED YOUR BOOK DOWN, SYD. I SPOKE TO MY EDITOR THERE ABOUT IT.

DAD, IT'S MORE COMPET-ITIVE NOW. NOT LIKE WHEN YOU WERE YOUNG AND ANY **HALF-WIT** COULD GET HIS DISSER-TATION PUBLISHED.

SYDNEY, YOU DIDN'T FAWN OVER PAUL'S OBSCENELY EX-PENSIVE NEW SWEATER.

NICE! I'VE ALWAYS WANTED A CASHMERE TURTLENECK.

I'LL GET YOU ONE TOMORROW. JENNI-FER ALREADY THINKS I SPEND TOO MUCH MONEY. A LITTLE MORE WON'T HURT.

HEY, ONE OF MY CRE-DIT CARDS RAISED MY LIMIT ANOTHER THOU! LET'S GO CHECK OUT THE NEW SKI EQUIPMENT, TOO.

SYDNEY! YOU CAN'T JUST BUY STUFF UNTIL YOU MAX OUT YOUR CREDIT! THAT'S INSANE!

AND LET'S GO BY GIZMO WORLD. I NEED A NEW PERSONAL DIGITAL ASSIS-TANT.

GREAT!

YOU SHOULD BE GLAD YOU TWO CAN'T GET MARRIED. WHEN SHE CRASHES AND BURNS, YOU WON'T BE LIABLE FOR HER DEBT.

Meanwhile, Ginger is off jobhunting at the Modern Language Association Convention.

LOIS! I GOT YOUR MESSAGE! IS DIGGER OKAY?

YEAH, EVERYTHING'S UNDER CONTROL. SHE WAS LIMPING WHEN I GOT HOME, SO I TOOK HER TO THE VET. THEY SAID SHE HAS RHEUMATISM AND TO GIVE HER IBUPROFEN.

Welcome to THE TORONTO COLONY HOTEL

GINGER, RELAX! I CANCELLED MY PLANS TO GO TO MY FOLKS SO I CAN STAY WITH HER ALL WEEKEND.

HEY, NO PROBLEM, BELIEVE ME. I JUMPED AT THE CHANCE.

OKAY. WAIT A SEC.

VICTORIA'S SECRET

SHE WANTS TO TALK TO YOU.

GIGGLE.

STOMP STOMP

GRRRR!

HEY, GINGER! SOUNDS LIKE SPARROW'S HOME. AND I THINK SHE MIGHT HAVE THE MYSTERY DATE IN TOW.

REALLY? WHO IS IT? WHAT'S SHE LOOK LIKE?

URF!

UH... KINDA LIKE RICHARD DREYFUSS IN "JAWS," ONLY BALDER.

LOIS! WHAT ARE YOU DOING HERE?

AR AR ARF!

39

the long goodbye

© 1997 BY ALISON BECHDEL

279

ALBERTA! BRING ME SOME OF THAT PORK GOULASH YOU ALL HAD FOR DINNER.

UH... OKAY, MAMA!

HOME SWEET HOME

XENA

YOU KNOW, ALBERTA... I MEAN JEZANNA. THAT'S WHAT YOU LIKE TO BE CALLED, ISN'T IT? I DON'T THINK I'VE EVER TOLD YOU HOW PROUD I AM OF YOU.

WHOA, MAMA! I THINK YOU'RE HAVING A WEIRD REACTION TO THE MORPHINE.

AND TAKE IT EASY ON THE GOULASH. YOU HAVEN'T EATEN IN WEEKS!

LORD KNOWS I'VE BEEN HARD ON YOU, GIRL. BUT THIS WORLD IS A HARD PLACE. I DIDN'T WANT YOU GROWING UP A FOOL, OR WORSE.

AND I DID RIGHT. LOOK AT YOU. YOU'RE A DAMN FINE DAUGHTER, EVEN IF YOU ARE A BULL-DAGGER.

MAMA!

NOW GET ME SOME TABASCO SAUCE.

YES, MA'M!

40

POOF!

MAMA?

MAMA.

MEANWHILE...

MOMMEEE!

SWEETIE, MOMMY HAS TO GO TO HER NEW JOB NOW. I EXPLAINED THAT TO YOU YESTERDAY WHEN WE VISITED THIS NICE PLACE.

RAINBOW PRESCHOOL

YOU'RE A BIG BOY, RAFFI! BIG BOYS GO TO SCHOOL. CARLOS WILL PICK YOU UP AT LUNCHTIME.

RAFFI! WOULD YOU LIKE TO PLAY WITH THE BEETLEBORGS?

DON'T GOOOO!

TOVAH   ETHAN   SAM   WILLOW

NOOOO!

DON'T WORRY. HE'LL BE FINE IN FIVE MINUTES.

IT'S NOT HIM I'M WORRIED ABOUT.

41

a Guy thing

Ginger returns from the MLA convention.

©1997 BY ALISON BECHDEL (280)

BABY!

YIP!

Harvest

United

TIP O' TH' NIB TO AMEY "FÜKENGRÜEN" RADCLIFFE

CAN YOU EVER FORGIVE YOUR SELFISH MOTHER FOR PUTTING HER CAREER FIRST AND LEAVING HER POOR L'IL RHEUMATIC PUPPY HOME ALL ALONE?

DIGGER, I TOLD YOU TO MAKE HER BEG.

...SUPPORT FOR NON-COMMERCIAL NATIONAL PUBLIC RADIO...

GOD, LOIS! IT'S COLDER HERE THAN IN TORONTO! DON'T YOU HAVE HEAT IN THIS THING?

NO, AND AT THE LEASE RATE I'M PAYING, MY DEALER'S GONNA HEAR ABOUT IT! SO, DIDJA GET A JOB?

SCRAPE SCRAPE

...COMES FROM THE ARCHER DANIELS MIDLAND COMPANY...

OH, I DUNNO...THE PRINCETON INTERVIEW WAS TOUGH, BUT I REALLY IMPRESSED BUFFALO LAKE STATE.

BUFFALO LAKE? YOU FLEW ALL THE WAY TO CANADA TO GET INTERVIEWED BY A RINKY-DINK SCHOOL TWO HOURS FROM HERE?

BONUS QUIZ! SPOT THE THREE PHRASES THAT **AREN'T** VERBATIM FROM ADM'S "NON-COMMERCIAL" ON NPR.

...MAKER OF GREEN GIANT HARVEST BURGERS...

ONE HOUR AND FORTY-FIVE MINUTES. TENURE TRACK. 28 THOU AND A KILLER SCHEDULE. AND SPEAKING OF HARSH REALITIES, ARE WE HOMELESS YET?

I DON'T THINK SO. THE REALTOR ONLY BROUGHT ONE BUYER THROUGH WHILE YOU WERE GONE.

...A GENETICALLY ALTERED SOY PROTEIN-BASED...

AND WHAT THE **HELL** IS UP WITH SPARROW?!

SHE'S SEEING THIS **GUY!**

...CHOLESTEROL-FREE ENTRÉE WITH FOUR GRAMS OF FAT, FOUND IN MOST SUPERMARKETS.

YEAH, BUT HOW **MUCH** OF HIM?

WELL, NOT THE WHOLE CHIMI-CHANGA, APPARENTLY. HE DIDN'T SLEEP OVER.

...ADM. INTERNATIONAL PRICE FIXING CONSPIRATOR...

A **MAN!** WHAT **IS** THIS? SOME KIND OF MIDLIFE CRISIS?!

...AMERICA'S BIGGEST CORPORATE WELFARE RECIPIENT...

I DUNNO. SHE WON'T TALK TO ME ABOUT IT. SHE'S PROBABLY AFRAID WE'LL DISAPPROVE.

REALLY? WELL **THAT'S** INSULTING! I DON'T HAVE A PROBLEM WITH MEN! AS LONG AS THEY DON'T WALK AROUND NAKED. OR GET THEIR BODY HAIR ALL OVER THE SOAP. OR TAKE UP A LOT OF SPACE. OR HAVE LOUD, BOOMING VOICES. OR...

...AND SUPERMARKET TO THE WORLD. THIS IS NPR.

YEAH, JEEZ. I CAN'T BELIEVE SPARROW WOULD THINK WE WERE THAT SMALL-MINDED.

life with father

© 1997 BY ALISON BECHDEL

TURNIP GREENS! TROTTERS! WHAT A **HEARTSTOPPING** SPREAD. WISH I STILL ATE MEAT. THE ONLY THING HERE I CAN HAVE ARE THE ROLLS.

DID I EVER TELL YOU ABOUT WANDA BARNES' GIRL THAT WENT VEGETARIAN? IN TWO WEEKS SHE WAS BALD AS A BILLIARD BALL.

281

A BIG TIP O' THE NIB TO BARBARA SMITH

SHE SHAVED HER HEAD, AUNT YOLANDA.

THAT'S WHAT SHE **TOLD** PEOPLE.

HI, BABY. HAS ETTA SETTLED DOWN?

I THINK SO. I NEVER SAW ANYONE GET THE SPIRIT QUITE AS POWERFULLY AS SHE DID TODAY.

TRUST ME. IT WOULDN'T'VE BEEN A CHURCH SERVICE IF ETTA HADN'T FALLEN OUT.

DON'T BE RUDE. SHE'S GOING TO BE LOOKING AFTER YOUR FATHER NOW.

LISTEN, I LOVE MY FAMILY, BUT I CAN'T WAIT TO GET BACK HOME. TO **OUR** HOME. ARE YOU REALLY COMING WITH ME? FOR GOOD?

I'D BETTER BE. I QUIT MY DAMN JOB.

ALBERTA! GO SAY GOODBYE TO THE PREACHER.

REVEREND, THANK YOU FOR THAT MOVING EULOGY. I HAD NO IDEA MY MOTHER GAVE SO MUCH TIME TO THE CHURCH BUILDING FUND.

SHE WAS A GENEROUS LADY. AND IT SOUNDS LIKE YOU TAKE RIGHT AFTER HER. YOUR FATHER JUST TOLD ME HE'S MOVING UP NORTH WITH YOU AND YOUR, UH...FRIEND AUDREY.

HE **WHAT?** KA-HACK!

THOSE ROLLS ARE AWFUL DRY. GO TRY SOME OF THAT CORNBREAD WITH THE HAM CHUNKS AND BACON DRIPPINGS.

Slap!

MEANWHILE...

OKAY, DAD, OKAY! NOW WILL YOU GET OFF MY ASS? GOODBYE!

NOW WHAT?

OH, HE WANTS ME TO SEND A CHAPTER OF MY BOOK TO SOME INFLUENTIAL OLD FART HE KNOWS.

YOU TWO HAVE TERRIBLE BOUNDARIES, SYDNEY. WHY DO YOU LET HIM GET INTO YOUR BUSINESS LIKE THAT?

I DUNNO. IT'S NOT THAT BIG A DEAL TO KEEP HIM HAPPY.

HE SENT YOU ANOTHER CHECK, DIDN'T HE?

HOW WOULD YOU LIKE A NEW SWEATER? THEY JUST GOT SOME NICE STRIPED ONES IN DOWN AT PAPAYA REPUBLIC.

divert & conquer

© 1998 BY ALISON BECHDEL

282

THE MAN'S CLEARLY A SEX ADDICT. HE'S OUT OF CONTROL. LYING, SUBORNING PERJURY...

IT'S THIS PURITANICAL CULTURE THAT'S THE PROBLEM. DO PEOPLE REALLY EXPECT SOMEONE WITH THE RUTHLESS LUST FOR POWER IT TAKES TO BECOME PRESIDENT TO SPEND EVENINGS AT HOME WITH HIS STAMP COLLECTION?

PEEPEE-GATE

SEMEN STAINS

BEVERLY HILLS

NORDIC TRICK

ABDOMINATOR

OH, PLEASE! YOU WOULDN'T BE QUITE SO INDULGENT IF IT WAS NEWT GINGRICH GETTING BLOWJOBS IN THE OVAL OFFICE.

THANK YOU FOR THAT IMAGE.

NY LITERARY AGENT

RITZ-CARLTON

HA! THEY GOT US, SYDNEY! THE WORLD IS TEETERING ON THE BRINK OF GLOBAL DEFLATION, AND HERE WE SIT PRATTLING ABOUT THE PRESIDENT'S PENIS!

CAN I HAVE A SCREW?

CNN RATINGS UP 40%

PARTS LIST

IS THIS GANNETT RAG SHOWING US HOW THE ASIAN BAILOUT BENEFITS BANKS AND CORPORATIONS, BUT DESTROYS LOCAL ECONOMIES? IS DAN RATHER EXPLAINING HOW THE I.M.F.'S STRATEGY ESCALATES THE PROBLEM OF CHEAP FOREIGN LABOR AND THREATENS U.S. WORKERS' JOBS? NO!

WHERE ARE THE PHILLIPS HEADS?

A TIP O' THE NIB TO CHRIS MOES

THE CORPORATE BEHEMOTHS WHO OWN THE NEWS **DISTRACT** US WITH PRESIDENTIAL PECCADILLOES WHILE THEY PROCEED TO **PILLAGE** THE **PLANET** WITH **IMPUNITY!**

GOOD POINT. WHILE YOU'RE UP, COULD YOU SEE IF I LEFT THOSE SCREWS BY THE PHONE?

YEAH, HERE THEY... UH... ARE.

PLATINUM card
Marlinecard

MISTRESS CARD

PREVIOUS BALANCE $11,462
PURCHASES 387.4
FINANCE CHARGE 203.9
LATE FEE 12
BALANCE $12,06

SYDNEY! THERE WAS THIS STACK OF CREDIT CARD BILLS LYING ON YOUR DESK! I... I'M SHOCKED! D'YOU REALLY OWE THIS MUCH MONEY?

UHH...

MO... I'M HAVING AN AFFAIR WITH ONE OF MY STUDENTS.

WHAT?!

IT JUST SORT OF HAPPENED. ONE MINUTE WE WERE DISCUSSING GENDER SLIPPAGE, AND THE NEXT, SHE'D SLIPPED RIGHT OUT OF HER AQUA PLAID STRETCH PANTS!

ARE YOU SERIOUS?

UNFORTUNATELY NOT. BUT FOR THE RECORD, YOUR DISTRACTION THEORY IS SOUND.

the iceman cometh

©1998 By Alison Bechdel

283

GINGER! THANK GOD YOU'RE HOME! I WAS SO WORRIED WHEN I HEARD THE WEATHER REPORT. HOW WERE THE ROADS?

FOUR HOURS TO DRIVE A HUNDRED MILES. I CAN'T UNCLENCH MY HANDS.

HOW'D IT GO AT BUFFALO LAKE STATE? ARE THEY GONNA HIRE YOU?

I HAVE A SINKING FEELING THEY MIGHT. SPARROW, YOU'RE NOT GOING **OUT** ARE YOU?

SHE PROBABLY HAS A DATE WITH HER GENTLEMAN CALLER.

WHAT'S IT FEEL LIKE TO BE STRAIGHT?

LOIS! I...I'M NOT STRAIGHT!

SO WHAT'RE YOU DOING WITH THIS GUY? TALK TO US! YOU'VE BEEN SNEAKING AROUND LIKE A GUILTY TEENAGER!

I DON'T **KNOW** WHAT I'M DOING! THIS IS VERY CONFUSING, AND YOU'RE NOT MAKING IT ANY EASIER.

ARE YOU SCHTUPPING HIM?

NO.

DO YOU WANT TO?

collateral DAMAGE

© 1998 BY ALISON BECHDEL

(284)

SₚARROW'S SWAIN APPEARS TO BE IN A MILD STATE OF SHOCK.

HERE. LIE DOWN AND ELEVATE YOUR FEET. I'LL GET YOU SOME HOT TEA WITH HONEY.

LOIS, COULD YOU FIND HIS TRIPLE A CARD IN HERE AND GET HIS CAR TOWED?

NO, I CAN DO IT. I'M F-F-FINE.

GIVE IT UP, STUART. WHO'S YOUR MECHANIC?

SHORTLY, IN THE KITCHEN...

RIGHT. WRAPPED AROUND A PHONE POLE AT 19TH AND MARTIN. WHY, THANK YOU, RITA. YOU HAVE A LOVELY EVENING TOO!

THIRTY-FOUR BUCKS CASH, AND THREE HUNDRED SEVENTY-ONE IN THE BANK. HUH. IF THAT'S STRAIGHT WHITE MALE PRIVILEGE, WE'RE NOT MISSING MUCH.

LOIS, YOU CAN'T JUST RIFLE THROUGH HIS WALLET!

CAN TOO. GROOVY P.C. CREDIT CARD, CO-OP MEMBERSHIP, THERAPIST'S BUSINESS CARD...JEEZ, MAYBE HE **IS** A LESBIAN.

PUT THAT STUFF BACK! HE'LL KNOW YOU WERE INTO IT!

WHITE HOUSE PREPARES PUBLIC FOR WAR IN IRAQ

WHAT DO YOU CARE? YOU'RE BEING SUSPICIOUSLY NICE TO THIS GUY. "OH, STUART! LET ME GET YOU SOME TEA!"

HEY, I'M JUST BEING POLITE. I'D DO THE SAME IF SPARROW WAS SEEING A WOMAN.

"IF WE'RE GONNA MURDER CIVILIANS, WE WANT POPULAR SUPPORT."

BUT SHE'S **NOT**, BLANCHE. SHE'S **NOT**. COME ON. I KNOW IT BUGS YOU. QUIT BEING SO TOLERANT.

WELL... I GUESS I AM DISAPPOINTED IN HER. IT'S JUST SO... **CONVENTIONAL**.

DON'TCHA FEEL LEFT IN THE LURCH? SHE'LL BE SHOWERED WITH APPROVAL AND APPLIANCES WHILE WE STAY HERE FENDING OFF **PROMISEKEEPERS** AND "PRO-FAMILY" **PREVERTS**.

YEAH. HER LIFE WILL BE COMPLETELY DIFFERENT WITH A MAN. A **WHITE** MAN AT THAT! WHAT IS SHE **THINKING**?

I DUNNO, BUT I FEEL **HAD**.

SPLORT!

YEAH, **BETRAYED**. SPARROW SEEING A GUY IS LIKE **CLINTON** TURNING OUT TO BE JUST ANOTHER HYPOCRITICAL, FAMILY VALUES SPEWING, WELFARE-SLASHING, SABER RATTLING **THUG**!

REALLY.

STU! DUDE, I GOT YOUR TEA!

object lesson

WHERE'S MOMMY?

SHE'S STILL AT WORK, SPORT. AUNT MO'S GONNA HELP US MAKE SUPPER.

IS THIS CAULIFLOWER ORGANIC?

285

Soy Slurp

I DUNNO. I JUST GRABBED IT. SO SYDNEY REALLY HAS 20 THOUSAND DOLLARS OF CREDIT CARD DEBT? HOW'S THAT EVEN POSSIBLE?

WHAT'S ORGANIC?

IT'S FOOD WITHOUT PESTICIDES IN IT, RAFFI.

WHAT'S PESTICIZE?

UH... POISON TO KILL BUGS WITH. SHE JUST KEPT GETTING MORE CARDS AND HIGHER LIMITS. SHE'S REALLY FREAKED OUT ABOUT IT, BUT THE WAY SHE MAKES HERSELF FEEL BETTER IS TO GO BUY MORE **STUFF**.

AH, THE BEAUTY OF CAPITALISM.

WHAT'S CAPITALISM?

YOU FIELD THAT ONE, MO. I GOTTA CHANGE.

Panel 1: WELL, RAFFI, CAPITALISM IS A WAY FOR RICH PEOPLE TO KEEP GETTING RICHER, NO MATTER WHAT THE COST. TAKE THIS CAULIFLOWER.

Panel 2: A RICH MAN PAYS UNLIVABLE WAGES TO MIGRANT WORKERS TO PLANT CAULIFLOWERS AND SPRAY THEM WITH **PESTICIDES.** THE WORKERS GET SICK FROM THE POISON, AND THE RESIDUE IN THE FOOD CAN CAUSE **BRAIN DAMAGE,** BUT CAPITALISM DOESN'T CARE!

THUNK!

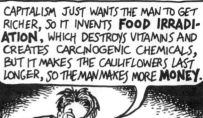

Panel 3: CAPITALISM JUST WANTS THE MAN TO GET RICHER, SO IT INVENTS **FOOD IRRADIATION,** WHICH DESTROYS VITAMINS AND CREATES CARCINOGENIC CHEMICALS, BUT IT MAKES THE CAULIFLOWERS LAST LONGER, SO THE MAN MAKES MORE **MONEY.**

CHOP!

Panel 4: **THEN** CAPITALISM FINDS A WAY TO **GENETICALLY ALTER** THE CAULIFLOWER SEEDS TO WITHSTAND THE WEED KILLER THE MAN **ALSO** HAPPENS TO SELL, SO HIS PROFITS **SKYROCKET.**

THWACKETA THWACKETA!

Panel 5: AT LAST, THE MAN IS SO RICH AND POWERFUL THAT IF ANYONE SUGGESTS HIS PESTICIDE-RIDDEN, IRRADIATED, GENETICALLY-MUTATED CAULIFLOWERS AREN'T **GOOD** FOR YOU, HE CAN SUE THEM FOR STILL **MORE** MONEY! **THAT'S** CAPITALISM. ANY QUESTIONS?

CAN WE GO TO BURGER KING? I DON'T LIKE CAULIFLOWERS.

Panel 6: UH, SWEETIE? REMEMBER WHAT I TOLD YOU ABOUT MENTIONING BURGER KING IN FRONT OF AUNT MO.

YEAH! IS SHE GONNA HAVE A STROKE NOW?

NOT JUST YET. I HAVE TO CALL CHILD PROTECTIVE SERVICES FIRST.

53

everything I need to know I learned from my four-year-old

(287)

© 1998 BY ALISON BECHDEL

Panel 1

SORRY WE'RE LATE. OH, GOOD. YOU GOT DINNER.

IT'S COLD BY NOW. I'VE JUST BEEN SITTING HERE READING THIS SICK EX-GAY LITERATURE YOUR MOTHER KEEPS SENDING US. WHAT'RE WE GONNA DO WITH HER?

PIZZA!

DESERT of the HEART MINISTRY

SUBMIT TA JESUS FAGS

Panel 2

ONE THING AT A TIME, BABE. I HAD TO STAY AND TALK TO PAULA AT THE PRESCHOOL BECAUSE THERE WAS SOME TROUBLE TODAY. TELL MEEMA WHAT YOU DID, RAFFI.

HIT SAM IN DA HEAD WIF DA TONKA CEMENT MIXER 'CAUSE HE WOULDN'T SHARE.

Panel 3

YOU HIT HIM WITH A **TRUCK?** RAFFI, YOU KNOW BETTER THAN THAT! WHAT GOT **INTO** YOU?

COULD WE TRY AND REMAIN CALM, PLEASE?

Panel 4

SORRY! I'M NOT FEELING CALM AT THE MOMENT!

SWEETIE, GO WASH YOUR HANDS.

Panel 5

CLARICE, YOU'VE GOT TO CONTROL YOUR ANGER. WHERE DO YOU THINK HE'S LEARNING TO ACT OUT LIKE THAT?

HIS BEHAVIOR UPSET ME, TONI, AND HE NEEDS TO KNOW THAT. I'M NOT GONNA ACT LIKE SOME LOBOTOMIZED MR. ROGERS.

57

WHERE IS
THE SLUSH
_of_
YESTERYEAR?

© 1998 BY ALISON BECHDEL

288

①NE SPRINGY SATURDAY MORNING...

FEMINISTS CAN'T WIN! IF WE CRITICIZE CLINTON'S BEHAVIOR, WE'RE PRUDES. AND IF WE SUGGEST HIS SEX LIFE IS HIS OWN BUSINESS, WE'RE HYPOCRITES. IT'S THE SAME OLD VIRGIN / WHORE TRAP.

WILLEY VS. WILLIE: N.O.W. SAYS PREZ COMMITTED ASSAULT

STEINEM SAYS GROPING BY BOSS OKAY IF HE'S A DEMOCRAT

ACTUALLY, I WAS JUST THINKING THAT ALL THIS OBSESSION WITH OUR FEARLESS LEADER'S WENCHING HAS HAD THE INTERESTING ANCILLARY FUNCTION OF EXPANDING THE DISCURSIVE DEMARCATIONS OF WOMEN'S SEXUAL SUBJECTIVITY.

WHAT?

ROUGH-AGE FLAKES

THE MORE OPEN DISCUSSION THERE IS ABOUT SEX, THE MORE WE MOVE BEYOND THE FALSE POLARITY OF WOMEN AS EITHER SEXUAL PREY, OR FRAIL VIRGINS IN NEED OF PROTECTION.

SOMEHOW, I THINK THAT POINT WILL ELUDE YOUR AVERAGE JOE MOLESTER. IF THIS IS PROGRESS, TAKE ME BACK TO THE FIFTIES. HEY! THAT'S THE LAST BANANA!

PUFFED GROATS

SENSING CHANGE IN CLIMATE, BOB PACKWOOD MAY RUN FOR OFFICE AGAIN

YOU WANT IT? COME AND GET IT!

SYDNEY! C'MON, I HAFTA GO TO WORK!

I'VE WANTED TO DO THIS EVER SINCE I LAID EYES ON YOU.

Forty-seven minutes later...

COMING SOON
BOUNDERS
BOOKS-N-MUZAK

UNDER CONSTRUCTION

BZZZZ

HEY, MO! CHECK IT OUT! IS THIS THE SHIT, OR WHAT?

WOW! YOU GOT INTO BROWN! CONGRATULATIONS, ANJALI!

MADWIMMIN BOOKS

I'M SO STOKED! I CAN'T DECIDE WHETHER I WANT TO CONCENTRATE IN MODERN CULTURE AND MEDIA, OR SEXUALITY AND SOCIETY. WHAT'D YOU MAJOR IN?

UM... GETTING HIGH AND COMING OUT, IF MEMORY SERVES.

SORRY I'M LATE, JEZ.

DOESN'T MATTER. HARDLY ANYONE'S BEEN IN. THEY'RE PROBABLY ALL AT BUNNS AND NOODLE, DUNKING BISCOTTI OVER THE LATEST GLOSSIES.

OFFICE

PUBLISHER'S WEAKLY
MEDIA CONGLOMERATE BERTELSMANN ACQUIRES RANDOM HOUSE

JEZANNA, DON'T BE SO NEGATIVE! WE'VE GOT LOYAL CUSTOMERS! WE'RE HANGING IN!

I'M GETTING TOO OLD FOR HANGING IN. I WORKED LIKE A DOG TO GET THIS PLACE STARTED. I NEVER THOUGHT I'D LOOK BACK ON THOSE DAYS AS MY GOLDEN YEARS.

SHRINKING COMPETITION SPELLS DOOM FOR CULTURAL LIFE OF NATION

GOD! YOU'RE SO APOCALYPTIC! ARE YOU, LIKE, MENOPAUSAL OR SOMETHING?

MO, ON THE OFF CHANCE A STRAY CUSTOMER **DOES** WANDER IN, COULD YOU GET THE HELL TO WORK?

59

deferred Interest

289

...AND WITH AN ADJUSTABLE RATE MORTGAGE, YOU WANT TO BE CAREFUL OF NEGATIVE AMORTIZATION, OR DEFERRED INTEREST, BECAUSE AT THE END OF THE YEAR, YOU COULD BE FURTHER IN DEBT THAN WHEN YOU STARTED.

GOD, MY HEAD'S SWIMMING. I'M SO GLAD WE'RE BUYING HOUSES AT THE SAME TIME. I DON'T KNOW IF I COULD FIGURE ALL THIS OUT ON MY OWN.

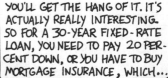

YOU'LL GET THE HANG OF IT. IT'S ACTUALLY REALLY INTERESTING. SO FOR A 30-YEAR FIXED-RATE LOAN, YOU NEED TO PAY 20 PERCENT DOWN, OR YOU HAVE TO BUY MORTGAGE INSURANCE, WHICH...

I THINK IT'S GREAT YOU'RE COMMITTED TO STAYING IN THE NEIGHBORHOOD, GINGER. I DON'T WANT TO LEAVE, BUT...

BUT WE DON'T WANT RAFFI GROWING UP NEXT DOOR TO A CRACK HOUSE.

OKAY. THE BEST DEAL IS A 15-YEAR LOAN. YOU END UP PAYING WAY LESS INTEREST, BUT OF COURSE THE MONTHLY PAYMENTS ARE HIGHER.

I DON'T THINK I COULD AFFORD THAT. BUFFALO LAKE IS ONLY GIVING ME A PITTANCE.

HOW'D YOU DECIDE TO TAKE THE JOB? DIDN'T YOU SAY TEACHING AT A MOSTLY WHITE, SMALL-TOWN STATE COLLEGE SOUNDED LIKE THE NINTH CIRCLE OF HELL?

WELL, HELL STARTED LOOKING PRETTY GOOD. IT'S NOT EXACTLY A BUYER'S MARKET OUT THERE. 463 PEOPLE APPLIED FOR THIS JOB!

LOOK WHAT I GOT, GINGER!

WHOA, RAFFI. THAT'S VERY UH... LETHAL LOOKING.

SO MUCH FOR 'NO MORE WAR TOYS.' SYDNEY GOT HIM THAT. SHE AND MO TOOK HIM TO TOYS R US LAST NIGHT WHILE I WAS AT A FREEDOM TO MARRY MEETING.

HEY, DO YOU HAVE ANY INTEREST IN VOLUNTEERING? IT'S SUCH IMPORTANT WORK!

UM... ACTUALLY, MARRIAGE ISN'T REAL HIGH ON MY AGENDA RIGHT NOW.

TONI, NOT EVERYONE WANTS TO FIGHT FOR THE DUBIOUS RIGHT OF HAVING THEIR DOMESTIC AFFAIRS LEGITIMIZED BY THE PATRIARCHY.

LISTEN, CLARICE, IT'S A MUCH MORE RADICAL ACT FOR TWO WOMEN TO CHALLENGE THE STATE BY GETTING MARRIED THAN TO SIT AROUND MUTTERING ABOUT THE PATRIARCHY.

UM... COULD YOU EXPLAIN THAT STUFF ABOUT "POINTS" AGAIN, AND HOW THEY AFFECT THE INTEREST RATE?

THWACK!

RAFFI!

LATER THAT EVENING...

I LOVE THAT WE'RE FRIENDS WITH GINGER. IT MAKES ME FEEL SO SOPHISTICATED, LIKE WE'RE IN A NOEL COWARD PLAY. WHEN WAS IT YOU TWO HAD THAT AFFAIR? TEN YEARS AGO?

CLARICE?

Real Estate Guide 121st century

61

LOVE and WORK

part 1

© 1998 BY ALISON BECHDEL

BUTCH IN THE STREETS, FEMME IN THE SHEETS? HOW **TOO** TRITE.

SIT BACK & HANG ON AS OUR SPECIAL 2-PART SERIES EXPLORES SOME **MORE PIQUANT** DISPARITIES BETWEEN WORKPLACE AND BEDROOM DEMEANOR.

(290)

AT WORK, CLARICE HAS LASERLIKE FOCUS,

YOUR HONOR, MY ESTEEMED COLLEAGUE IS OVERLOOKING SECTION 304 (a) AND (f), 42 U.S.C. SEC. 7604, WHICH SETS AN EMISSION LIMIT OF 5μg/m³ OVER ANY 30 DAY PERIOD, IF I'M NOT MISTAKEN.

WHICH I'M NOT.

...AND TONI EXUDES MATURITY.

BECAUSE I'M THE EXECUTIVE DIRECTOR, THAT'S WHY!

JOAN, LET'S DISCUSS THIS AFTER LUNCH. YOU KNOW YOU GET IRRITABLE WHEN YOU'RE HUNGRY.

TONI ORTIZ, BUS. MGR.

BUT IN THE BOUDOIR...

HA! I TAPED THIS FOR RAFFI, BUT IT'S REALLY GROWING ON ME.

HUH?

AGAIN!

AT THE BOOKSTORE, JEZANNA IS A WOMAN OF FEW WORDS,

DIDJA SEE BOUNDERS BOOKS AND MUSIC IS HAVING THEIR GRAND OPENING NEXT MONTH?

OFFICE

MMPH.

... BUT IN AN INTIMATE SETTING, SHE'S A BIT MORE VOLUBLE.

OH, **WHERE**'D YOU LEARN TO **DO** THAT? **YES!** DON'T **STOP!** @*#! ME, YOU *$@¢!

BABE, BEFORE YOUR FATHER MOVES IN, WE NEED TO TALK SOUNDPROOFING.

LOVE and WORK part II

© 1998 BY ALISON BECHDEL

TO LOVE AND TO WORK. THE TWIN CONDITIONS OF A MEANINGFUL LIFE. BUT IS OUR PERFORMANCE IN ONE ARENA AN INDEX OF OUR PERFORMANCE IN THE OTHER?

JOIN US AS WE SEEK THE ANSWER IN THIS FINAL INSTALLMENT OF OUR PENETRATING INVESTIGATIVE SERIES.

291

SPARROW'S A MODEL OF DECISIVENESS DOWN AT THE SHELTER...

MARLENE'S KIDS NEED TO BE PICKED UP AND I CAN'T FIND A CAR.

No hitting

THE NEXT HOTLINE VOLUNTEER'S NOT HERE AND I HAVE TO LEAVE.

TAKE MINE.

THIS WOMAN'S HUSBAND'S VIOLATING HIS RELIEF FROM ABUSE ORDER AND THE POLICE AREN'T RESPONDING.

TELL HER TO INSIST ON SPEAKING TO DETECTIVE CATALANO.

JOANNE CAN COVER. TELL HER TO FORGET PLUNGING THE TOILET.

TIPS O'THE NIB TO PATTI MCMANAMY & NAT GRANT

AND STUART'S FUNDRAISING ZEAL IS UNFLAGGING.

FOOD FOR OLD PEOPLE? WE HERE AT THE GOLIATH HEALTH PLAN HAVE NEVER FUNDED ANYTHING LIKE THAT IN THE PAST.

DID YOU KNOW EVERY DOLLAR SPENT ON ELDER NUTRITION SAVES $3.25 IN HOSPITAL COSTS? CONSIDER YOUR BOTTOM LINE, MR. FLACK!

BUT IN THE RACK, SHE CAN'T DECIDE,

OKAY. LET'S DO IT.

ARE YOU SURE?

NO, WAIT.

UH... OKAY.

IT'S SO WEIRD TO THINK I COULD GET PREGNANT DOING THIS. MAYBE YOU SHOULD PUT ON ANOTHER CONDOM.

I DON'T THINK A FOURTH ONE WILL FIT!

... AND HE FINALLY FLAGS.

IS SOMETHING WRONG?

JEEZ... SORRY. THIS HAS NEVER HAPPENED TO ME BEFORE.

Trojans

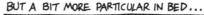

THEA'S EASYGOING ON THE JOB...

SHIT! I'M SORRY! I UNPLUGGED THE COMPUTER BY MISTAKE!

OH, DON'T WORRY. IT'S NOTHING I CAN'T RE-INPUT.

IN A WEEK.

BUT A BIT MORE PARTICULAR IN BED...

OKAY. CAT'S IN, DOOR'S LOCKED, PHONE'S OFF, IRON'S UNPLUGGED, CANDLE'S LIT, "BOLERO" IS CUED UP ON THE CD PLAYER. I GUESS WE'RE ALL SET.

DID YOU CLIP YOUR TOENAILS?

DISORIENTED BY HIS PROLONGED UNEMPLOYMENT, CARLOS IS HAVING SEX WHEN HE SHOULD BE WORKING...

"MIDNIGHT PLOWBOY"

...AND VICE VERSA.

OF COURSE I STILL LOVE YOU. I JUST HAVE TO GET THIS RESUMÉ OUT TOMORROW.

THAT'S ODD. WASN'T THIS NEARLY FULL ON SUNDAY?

AND LOIS BRINGS TO BOTH WORK AND PLAY...

THIS MODEL REALLY ROCKS IF IT FITS BOTH PEOPLE RIGHT.

THE ULTIMATE ANAL GUIDE TO SEX FOR WOMEN

DIESEL GRUEL POIMS

A CONSISTENT, SERVICE-ORIENTED APPROACH.

HOW'S THIS ANGLE FOR YOU?

I'LL TAKE IT. DO YOU GIFT WRAP?

an embarassment of condiments

©1998 BY ALISON BECHDEL

292

I HOPE YOU'RE NOT STARVING. TONI ISN'T BACK FROM HER FTM MEETING YET.

OH, TONI'S TRANSITIONING? HERE'S MORE RELISH. I DIDN'T KNOW YOU ALREADY HAD SOME.

NOT FEMALE-TO-MALE! FREEDOM TO MARRY. HERE'S SOME FRUIT-SWEETENED CATSUP.

PICNIC CHARK BIQUES

RELISH RELISH

PISS-N-VINEGAR CHIPS

SYDNEE!

COMMANDER SKYWALKER! QUICK! SAND PEOPLE ON THE NORTH RIDGE!

UH...HI, RAFFI.

SHOULD HE BE PLAYING WITH THAT LIGHT SABER? I MEAN, AREN'T YOU CONCERNED ABOUT ALL THESE BOYS MOWING DOWN THEIR CLASSMATES WITH ASSAULT RIFLES?

SQUEAL!

THANKS FOR YOUR CONCERN, MO. I'M NOT THE ONE WHO **BOUGHT** HIM THE DAMN THING.

HEY, I DID EVERYTHING I COULD TO TALK SYDNEY OUT OF IT. BUT SHE'S A **JUGGERNAUT** WHEN SHE'S GOT A VISA CARD IN HER HAND.

CHARCON

SHE STILL RACKING UP DEBT?

YEAH. IT'S LIKE SHE **HAS** TO HAVE NEW STUFF ALL THE TIME. HER CLOSET IS LIKE A J. SCREW WAREHOUSE!

Brigg

REALLY. UM, LISTEN, MO. I NEED TO TALK TO YOU BEFORE TONI GETS HERE...

WHAT'S GOING ON**?!** IS SOMETHING WRONG? YOU GUYS AREN'T BREAKING **UP,** ARE YOU?

GOD! NO! WILL YOU JUST LISTEN? REMEMBER HOW YEARS AGO I HAD THAT THING WITH GINGER? WELL, I'VE BEEN THINKING ABOUT HER A LOT LATELY...

THINKING AS IN MUSING, OR THINKING AS IN ENTERTAINING FEVERISH SEXUAL FANTASIES**?**

UM... THE LATTER.

GOD, CLARICE! YOU HAVEN'T SAID ANYTHING TO HER, HAVE YOU?

SKRITCH

OF **COURSE** NOT! WHAT'S COME OVER ME**?!** IT MUST BE SOME KIND OF **BACKLASH.** WE'RE BUYING A HOUSE, LEAVING THE NEIGHBORHOOD, TONI'S ON THIS "RIGHT TO MARRY" KICK**!** WE USED TO JOKE ABOUT BEING WARD AND JUNE CLEAVER, BUT IT'S NOT FUNNY ANYMORE. I'M SO **CLAUSTROPHOBIC,** I'M **CHOKING!**

HI! SORRY I'M LATE! I STOPPED BY THE CO-OP FOR BUNS, AND LOOK WHO I FOUND!

UM... HEY.

HEY,..UH.. I BROUGHT SOME RELISH.

I THINK ONE CAN SAFELY SAY THERE'S ENTIRELY TOO MUCH RELISH AT THIS BARBECUE.

home economics

© 1998 BY ALISON BECHDEL

IN A BRISK DOWNTOWN EATERY...

GINGER! WHAT ARE YOU DOING HERE?

HEY! JOIN ME! I WAS JUST OVER AT FIRST NATIONAL APPLYING FOR A MORTGAGE.

293

HOW'D IT GO?

NOT SO GOOD. THEY ASKED FOR A LOT MORE DOCUMENTATION THAN I WAS EXPECTING. AND THEY SAID IT LOOKS LIKE MY INCOME MIGHT NOT BE ENOUGH TO QUALIFY.

SURPRISE, SURPRISE.

YEAH. WHERE ARE YOU GETTING YOUR MORTGAGE?

I APPLIED WITH FIRST NATIONAL TOO, BUT I'VE BEEN MANAGING TO DO IT ALL OVER THE PHONE. USING MY BEST KATIE COURIC IMPERSONATION, I MIGHT ADD. IT'S BEEN GOING LIKE CLOCKWORK.

HUH. I DON'T THINK I COULD DO THAT. IF THEY'RE A BUNCH OF RACISTS, I WANNA KNOW ABOUT IT.

THE HORSE BLITH-ERER

YEAH, I CAN SEE THAT. YOU HAVE NO PRETENSE ABOUT YOU. IT'S VERY, UH... ATTRACTIVE.

...SO THEN I ALMOST SAID SOMETHING ABOUT HER **EYES**, BUT THAT'S WHEN CARLOS CAME OVER, THANK GOD!

WOW. YOU'RE REALLY 'ROUND THE BEND, BABE. TOO BAD SPARROW'S STILL SHACKING UP WITH STUART. SHE'D KNOCK SOME SENSE INTO YOU.

Strap-on Tools

GOD, I WISH SHE'D COME HOME. I DON'T CARE IF SHE BRINGS A WHOLE **HIVE** OF BOYFRIENDS WITH HER.

YEAH. IT MIGHT BE NICE HAVING A GUY AROUND THE HOUSE. MAYBE HE COULD SCORE ME SOME **VIAGRA**.

MEANWHILE...

YEAH, I KNOW. CLARICE CALLED EARLIER AND MENTIONED RUNNING INTO GINGER AT LUNCH.

SHE DID, HUH? AND DID SHE ALSO MENTION THE **SCORCHING GAZE** THEY WERE EXCHANGING?

WHAT ARE YOU SAYING, CARLOS?

I'M SAYING I MAY BE USELESS AT FINDING MYSELF A JOB, BUT I AM NEVER WRONG ABOUT AFFAIRS OF THE HEART. YOU KEEP AN EYE ON THAT GIRL.

WEEOOOWEEEOOWE

OH, EVERYTHING IS SEXUAL TO YOU. YOU'VE BEEN WATCHING TOO MUCH PORN.

MAYBE IF YOU WATCHED **MORE**, QUERIDA, YOU'D LEARN HOW TO KEEP HER AT HOME.

OOOWEEEOOOWEE

BALM BLAST

©1998 BY ALISON BECHDEL

Panel 1: THIS IS NICE. WE DON'T SPEND ENOUGH TIME TOGETHER. UM... SO, ARE YOU GONNA DRAW UP THAT SPENDING PLAN TODAY? YOU KNOW, TO GET YOUR DEBT UNDER CONTROL?

294

Panel 2: I CAN'T THINK ABOUT IT RIGHT NOW. THE ANTIHISTAMINES ARE STARTING TO KICK IN.

Panel 3: HEY! I JUST HEARD A NEW CAT ALLERGY SOLUTION! APPLY **TIGER BALM** AROUND YOUR EYES! I HAVE AN OLD TIN SOMEWHERE IF YOU...

Panel 4: I DON'T THINK SO. I RATHER LIKE BEING ABLE TO SEE.

HEIL STYLE!

Panel 5: GOD! HAVE YOU READ ABOUT THIS "**MILLENIUM MARCH**" BROUHAHA? THE HUMAN RIGHTS CAMPAIGN AND THE METROPOLITAN COMMUNITY CHURCH GOT TOGETHER AND UNILATERALLY DECIDED TO THROW A NATIONAL MARCH ON WASHINGTON IN 2000.

Panel 6: A TIDY, CLOSED-PROCESS, TOP-DOWN EXECUTIVE DECISION. NO PUBLIC MEETING, NO DISCUSSION WITH OTHER GAY AND LESBIAN ORGANIZATIONS, NO COORDINATION WITH OTHER PROGRESSIVE GROUPS.

ABSOLUT TWADDLE

OUT POST-GAY! THE NEW IDEOLOGY FOR FALL!

Panel 7: THE THEME IS "**FAITH AND FAMILY.**" GAG ME WITH A RAINBOW FLAG! OR A **CRUCIFIX!** THAT'S PROBABLY THE LOGO, A RAINBOW CRUCIFIX! I BET THEY'RE PRINTING IT ON SOUVENIR DIAPER BAGS AS WE SPEAK!

SEND MONEY PLEASE!

Panel 8: WELL, IF THE MESSAGE THAT WE'RE ALL CHURCHGOING MALL PATRONS WINS US MORE SUPPORT, MAYBE IT'S A GOOD STRATEGY FOR THE MOVEMENT.

IN

it's a
lifestyle
choice

©1998 BY ALISON BECHDEL

SPARROW IS STILL SOJOURNING AT STUART'S...

GOD! THAT NEW NEIGHBOR'S DRIVING ME **INSANE!** HE'S PLAYED THIS MÖTLEY CRÜE ALBUM SIX TIMES SINCE I GOT HOME! AND IS THAT **CIGAR SMOKE?!**

POOR BABY. SEE YOU LATER. I'M HAVING DINNER WITH LOIS AND GINGER.

Girls, Girls, Girls! ♪

295

SHORTLY...

THANKS FOR COMING, SPARROW. I'VE MISSED YOU SO MUCH.

HOW'S IT GOING, BABE?

GOOD! I MISS YOU GUYS TOO. I'M FEELING MUCH CLEARER ABOUT THINGS WITH STUART, AND I'M READY TO COME BACK.

EXCELLENT! ACTUALLY, THAT'S WHAT WE WANTED TO TALK TO YOU ABOUT.

NOW WHAT? HAVE YOU INSTITUTED VISITING HOURS FOR MALE GUESTS?

HEY, STU CAN MOVE IN AS FAR AS WE'RE CONCERNED. WE JUST WANT YOU TO CO-SIGN THE MORTGAGE AND SHELL OUT FIVE THOU TO HELP BUY THIS PLACE.

WHAT?

TURNS OUT GINGER CAN'T AFFORD THE HOUSE ON HER OWN.

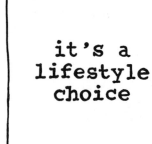

AND MY CREDIT ISN'T SO GOOD SINCE I DEFAULTED ON MY STUDENT LOAN.

COME ON! IT'S A GOOD INVESTMENT! AND NOT JUST FINANCIALLY!

IT'S AN INVESTMENT IN **FRIENDSHIP!** A COMMITMENT TO SHARING RESOURCES! A TRIUMPHANT BLOW TO THE ALIENATING CORPORATE FORCES THAT ARE STEADILY ERODING HUMAN BONDS!

OKAY. WHAT THE HELL. I'VE GOT SOME MONEY SAVED UP.

! REALLY?

REALLY. I'VE BEEN GIVING A LOT OF THOUGHT LATELY TO HOW I WANT TO LIVE. IT'S BEEN NICE STAYING AT STUART'S AND HAVING SOME PRIVACY. BUT THAT'S NOT WHAT I WANT PERMANENTLY, THAT KIND OF ISOLATED, COUPLE-FOCUSED EXISTENCE, ALL CUT OFF FROM THE WORLD.

*M*EANWHILE, IN A DIFFERENT ZIP CODE...

...AND WITH THE ELECTRIC GARAGE DOOR OPENER, YOU DON'T HAVE TO GET OUT OF YOUR CAR TO GO INSIDE!

UH... I THINK WE'RE LOOKING FOR SOMETHING A LITTLE LESS...UH...

HERMETICALLY SEALED.

Century 21
FOR SALE

*L*ATER THAT EVENING...

HI. LISTEN, I'M GONNA STAY HERE TONIGHT.... I KNOW. ME TOO...WHAT?...WELL, I GUESS SO. BUT I DON'T THINK IT'S VERY HEALTHY IF YOU CAN'T BE AWAY FROM ME FOR EVEN ONE NIGHT.

UH... I DO MISS YOU, BUT THAT'S NOT WHY I WANT TO COME OVER.

Girls, Girls, Girls! ♪ ♪♪

MACANUDO EXHAUST

I DON'T CARE IF HE'S DEAD. I STILL WANT TO IMPEACH NIXON

73

living
arrangements

© 1998 BY ALISON BECHDEL

ARE YOU INTERESTED?

ARE YOU MAKING ME AN OFFER?

296

CLARICE! WILL YOU PAY ATTENTION?

HUH?

I WAS JUST SAYING THAT IF YOU'RE REALLY INTERESTED IN THIS HOUSE, I ADVISE MAKING AN OFFER TODAY.

THWACK!

I THINK WE SHOULD DO IT. THIS ONE FEELS RIGHT TO ME.

WELL, SURE, IT **LOOKS** OKAY. BUT WHAT ABOUT THE PROBLEMS WE CAN'T SEE? LEAD PAINT, AIRPLANE NOISE..

...FUNDA-MENTALISTS, RADON...

HOW MUCH OF A DEPOSIT DO WE NEED TO PUT DOWN?

MEANWHILE,...

Grand Opening FREE CAPPUCCINO!

BOUNDERS BOOKS-N-MUZAK

TOM CLANCY

MO! WHAT ARE **YOU** DOING HERE?

OH, UH... HI, HARRIET. HI, CARLOS. JUST A LITTLE RESEARCH. YOU KNOW. GOTTA STAY ABREAST OF THE COMPETITION.

LOOKIN' PRESIDENTIAL: CLINTON BOMBS BEJEEZUS OUT OF SUDANESE PENICILLIN PLANT

WELL, I'M NO BOOK MAVEN LIKE YOURSELF, BUT I THINK THE JOE'S BETTER AT BUNNS AND NOODLE.

I HOPE YOU'RE NOT SPENDING ANY MONEY HERE.

RELAX! WE'RE JUST HAVING FREE DRINKS AND GOSSIPING.

Newswe EX-GAY? OR JUST BADLY DRESSED?

GOSSIPING? ABOUT WHO?

IS SYDNEY REALLY MOVING IN WITH YOU?

AND IS IT BECAUSE SHE'S IN SO MUCH DEBT SHE CAN'T PAY HER RENT?

Y'KNOW, IT'S VERY SAD TO SEE GROWN ADULTS TAKING SUCH AN INAPPROPRIATE INTEREST IN THE PRIVATE CONCERNS OF OTHER PEOPLE.

 AND MEANWHILE AGAIN...

WELL, THE GOOD NEWS IS, WE GOT THE MORTGAGE. THE BAD NEWS IS, WE'VE GOTTA REWIRE THE HOUSE BEFORE WE CAN BUY IT. SEEMS THINGS AREN'T QUITE UP TO CODE.

GREAT. WHERE ARE WE GONNA GET THE CABBAGE TO PAY FOR THAT? TAKE IN **LODGERS**?

THAT WAS STUART ON THE PHONE. YOU DON'T MIND IF HE STAYS OVER AGAIN, DO YOU? HIS NEIGHBOR SEEMS TO BE HAVING ANOTHER KEG PARTY.

WHATEVER. HE PRACTICALLY LIVES HERE ANYWAY.

STRAY VOLTAGE

©1998 BY ALISON BECHDEL

297

WOW. YOU'RE ONLY WIRED FOR SIXTY AMPS. LOTTA RODENT DAMAGE TOO, I'M SURPRISED THIS PLACE HASN'T BURNED TO THE GROUND.

UH... REALLY?

FUSES

SO, CAN YOU GIVE US AN ESTIMATE?

LEMME GO OUT TO THE TRUCK AND WORK IT UP.

IN A MOMENT...

LOOK, I'M NOT ASKING STUART TO MOVE IN. I'M NOT READY FOR THAT KIND OF COMMITMENT. I DON'T CARE HOW BADLY WE NEED THE MONEY.

SPARROW, THIS IS NO TIME FOR INTIMACY ISSUES. JUST THINK OF IT AS HAVING A TEMPORARY ROOMMATE TILL WE PAY OFF THE REPAIRS.

DON'T LECTURE **ME** ABOUT INTIMACY ISSUES. YOU'RE THE ONE OBSESSED WITH A MARRIED WOMAN. AT LEAST STUART IS **AVAILABLE!**

WHY DON'T YOU ASK **CLARICE** TO MOVE IN, GINGER. YOU'RE GENERATING ENOUGH ELECTRICITY WITH YOUR CRUSH, WE WON'T **NEED** TO REWIRE.

MEANWHILE...

THANKS FOR THE BOXES, MO. TONI'LL CREAM. SHE'S SO EXCITED ABOUT THE MOVE, SHE'S DEVELOPING A CARDBOARD FETISH.

MADWIMMIN BOOKS

NAIAD

76

YOU DON'T LOOK SO THRILLED.

I'M A WRECK. I'M THINKING ABOUT GINGER ALL THE TIME. IT'S CRAZY. I'M AFRAID TONI KNOWS SOMETHING'S WRONG.

THUNK!

CLARICE, YOU'VE GOTTA RECONCILE YOUR FEELINGS ABOUT LEAVING THE NEIGHBORHOOD. IT'S NOT GINGER YOU'RE ATTRACTED TO, IT'S WHAT SHE REPRESENTS. THE CO-OP, THE PARK, THE BLOCK FESTIVAL, THE COMMUNITY!

OH. SO IT'S REALLY THE COMMUNITY'S INNER THIGHS I WANT TO DRIZZLE WITH MAPLE CRÈME ANGLAISE, WHICH I THEN SLOWLY LAP UP WHILE STRADDLING THE TANTALIZING TONGUE OF THE CO-OP.

UH... WELL, SORT OF...

MEANWHILE, IN ST. LOUIS, JEZANNA AND AUDREY ARE PACKING UP JEZ'S FATHER TO COME BACK AND LIVE WITH THEM.

IT'S BEEN LONELY WITHOUT YOUR MAMA. BUT I'M GONNA MISS THIS HOUSE.

YOU CAN STILL CHANGE YOUR MIND. WE HAVEN'T SOLD IT YET, AND I CAN ALWAYS RETURN THE U-HAUL.

NUDGE

UH... LOTTA MEMORIES HERE, HUH, DAD?

REMEMBER THIS BURN MARK ON THE BASEBOARD, FROM THE TIME YOU STUCK THAT PIECE OF ERECTOR SET IN THE OUTLET? YOU WERE ALWAYS POKING INTO SOMETHING.

MMM, GIRL!

BACK AT THE RANCH...

OF COURSE, THAT DOESN'T INCLUDE REPAIRING THE WALLS AFTER I'M DONE.

Y'KNOW, MAYBE MY RELUCTANCE TO COMMIT IS A TAD UNHEALTHY.

$525 INCLUDING UTILITIES.

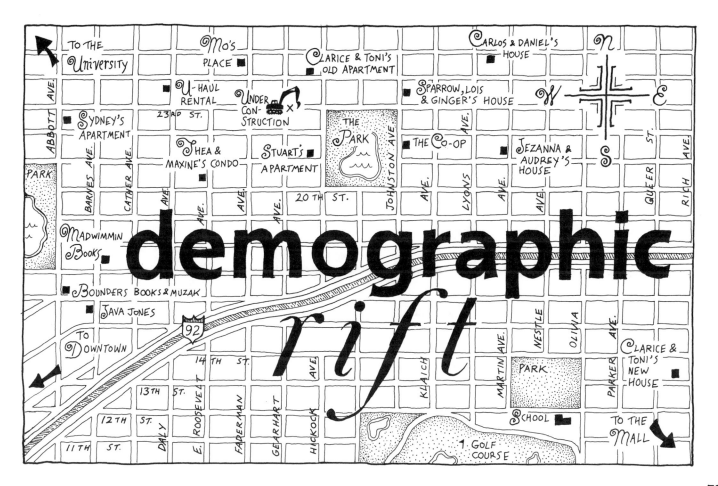

demographic *rift*

I THOUGHT WE'D LET RAFFI SLEEP LONGER, THEN YOU CAN FINISH PACKING HIS ROOM WITH HIM JUST BEFORE WE LEAVE FOR THE CLOSING. DID YOU SEE YOUR LIST?

WHEN DID YOU WRITE THIS? YOU MUST HAVE BEEN UP TILL THREE.

I NEVER WENT TO BED. I DON'T KNOW HOW YOU COULD SLEEP WHEN THERE'S SO MUCH TO THINK ABOUT. I PLANNED THE WHOLE DAY OUT IN FIFTEEN-MINUTE INCREMENTS. **SOMEONE** HAS TO BE ORGANIZED.

TONI? I DIDN'T SAY ANYTHING WHEN YOU MADE THE CROSS-REFERENCED LIST OF WHICH BOX EACH ITEM IS PACKED IN, BUT DON'T YOU THINK YOU'RE GETTING A LITTLE **OBSESSIVE**? WHAT'S GOING ON? WHY'RE YOU SO ANXIOUS?

CLARICE, WE DON'T HAVE TIME FOR A THERAPY SESSION. WILL YOU GET DRESSED?

STUFF STUFF

WHERE'S MY BACKHOE?

OH, SWEETIE. I PACKED IT UP TO TAKE TO THE NEW HOUSE. YOU CAN HAVE IT TONIGHT, AFTER WE MOVE.

GINGER! THE ELECTRICIAN'S HERE. SHE'S GONNA TURN THE POWER OFF.

YO! CATH! BRING IN THE **SAWZALL**, WOULDJA?

I COULD GO FOR A LITTLE BUTCH-ON-BUTCH ACTION WITH A STRAPPING LASS LIKE THAT. QUITE A **TOOLBELT**.

HOW NICE FOR YOU.

I CLEARED A SPOT IN THE BASEMENT FOR STUART'S STUFF. IN CASE IT DOESN'T ALL FIT UP HERE.

I CAN'T BELIEVE WE'RE GONNA HAVE A FOURTH PERSON LIVING IN THIS PLACE. LET ALONE A MAN. I JUST HOPE HE'S NOT A COMPLETE SLOB.

YEAH. THAT WOULD REALLY BE A PROBLEM CONSIDERING WE'RE ALL SO FASTIDIOUS. GOD, THERE ARE **BARNACLES** GROWING IN HERE!

◎ AND AT STUART'S APARTMENT...

UM... COULDN'T YOU FIND ANY BOXES?

I FIGURED WE COULD JUST USE THESE SHOPPING BAGS.

GRAND ONION

SO, WE'RE REALLY DOING IT, HUH?

MOVING IN TOGETHER? UM... YEAH. WHY? ARE YOU HAVING SECOND THOUGHTS?

I DON'T KNOW. I GUESS IT'S THE LESBIAN THING. ARE YOU REALLY SURE YOU WANT TO GET INVOLVED WITH ME?

WELL, I LOOK AT IT THIS WAY. IF I GET INVOLVED WITH SOMEONE WHO ALREADY **KNOWS** SHE'S A LESBIAN THEN IT WON'T COME AS A BIG SURPRISE TWO OR THREE YEARS DOWN THE LINE, LIKE IT DID WITH LILITH. AND ANN MARIE, AND SIGRID, AND...

MEANWHILE, 800 MILES AWAY...

I'LL HAVE SOME WRECKED HEN FRUIT, SWEEP THE KITCHEN, AND A SHINGLE, HOLD THE COW.

DINER

HUH?

HUH?! YOU WOULDN'T HAVE LASTED LONG AT **MY** DINER, YOUNG LADY. RAN MY OWN PLACE FOR 40 YEARS, AND I NEVER...

JUST BRING HIM SOME SCRAMBLED EGGS, A PLATE OF HASH, AND TOAST, NO BUTTER.

WHAT-EVER.

Panel 1: DAD, WE'VE GOT A LONG WAY TO GO, AND I HAVE TO GET THE TRUCK BACK BY 6:30 TONIGHT. LET'S JUST EAT BREAKFAST AND HOLD THE LIFE HISTORY, OKAY?

JEZANNA, LET THE MAN TALK TO THE WAITRESS.

Panel 2: IGNORE HER, ALBERT. SHE'S ALWAYS ORNERY BEFORE HER COFFEE KICKS IN.

YOU WANT SOME FINE COFFEE, THERE'S A PLACE I REMEMBER UP ALONG ROUTE 78. WE'LL GO RIGHT BY IT IF WE DON'T TAKE THE INTERSTATE.

Panel 3: ⊙ MEANWHILE...

HEY! GREEN MEANS **GO**, YOU PRO-LIFE PINHEAD!

UH... TONI? YOU SEEM A LITTLE ON EDGE.

Honnk! Broof

Panel 4: MO, I'M **BUYING** A **HOUSE** TODAY! ON THOSE STRESS CHARTS, THAT'S LIKE, SECOND ONLY TO LOSING YOUR SPOUSE OR SOMETHING.

IS, UH... EVERYTHING OKAY WITH YOU AND CLARICE?

Panel 5: OH, YEAH. HUNKY DORY. WE'RE ON THE VERGE OF SIGNING A 30-YEAR MORTGAGE AND SHE'S GOT ONE FOOT OUT THE DOOR.

OH, TONI. CLARICE PANICS EVERY TIME THE COMMITMENT ANTE GETS UPPED. BUT SHE ALWAYS COMES THROUGH IN THE END, DOESN'T SHE?

WELL, NOW THAT YOU MENTION IT, I GUESS SHE'S **ALWAYS** HAD ONE FOOT OUT THE DOOR. BUT SHE **IS** STILL HERE. MAYBE I SHOULD HAVE MORE FAITH IN HER. LIGHTEN UP A LITTLE, CALM DOWN. EVERYTHING'LL WORK OUT, RIGHT?

RIGHT. BELIEVE ME, THIS THING WITH GINGER WILL BLOW OVER.

WHAT THING WITH GINGER?!

SHIT! TONI, NO! THERE'S NOTHING GOING ON! I DIDN'T MEAN TO...

OH, RELAX. IT'S NOT LIKE I DIDN'T KNOW.

OH! SO YOU'VE TALKED ABOUT IT, THEN?

NO! I DON'T WANT TO MAKE A BIGGER DEAL OUT OF IT THAN IT ALREADY IS. BESIDES, I DON'T HAVE TIME TO PROCESS. THIS MOVE REQUIRES MY **COMPLETE FOCUS!**

U-HAUL

¡MIERDA! WE'RE THREE MINUTES LATE!

UH... SORRY. WELL, HERE WE ARE.

OKAY. WE'RE ON A **VERY** TIGHT SCHEDULE. YOU AND SYDNEY HAVE THE TRUCK TILL NOON. THEN YOU TAKE IT TO STUART'S. HE HAS TWO HOURS TO MOVE HIS STUFF TO SPARROW'S, THEN YOU DRIVE IT BACK HERE **NO LATER** THAN **2 O'CLOCK.** IF YOU'RE A **NANOSECOND** LATE, YOU'LL FUCK EVERYTHING UP!

TONI, IT'S GONNA BE FINE!

Lurch!

Stall...

PARKING BRAKE! SORRY!

CLARICE! I'M BACK! LET'S GO!

¡HOLA, QUERIDA! SHE JUST GOT OUT OF THE SHOWER.

CARLOS! GOOD, YOU'RE HERE. I NEED TO GO OVER A FEW THINGS WITH YOU.

I WANT YOU TO SUPERVISE THE MOVERS WHEN THEY COME FOR THE BIG FURNITURE. I DON'T WANT THEM BUMPING STUFF AROUND. MAKE SURE THEY USE BLANKETS ON THE DRESSER. AND DON'T LET THEM SMOKE IN HERE. CAN YOU DO THAT?

UM... OKAY.

TONI, WHY AREN'T WE HAVING THE MOVERS TAKE EVERYTHING? IT'D BE A LOT EASIER THAN RENTING A TRUCK AND MAKING ALL OUR FRIENDS HAUL BOXES.

A.) IT'S TOO EXPENSIVE, AND B.) IT'S ALREADY PLANNED.

YOU BETTER RUN ALONG TO THE CLOSING. YOU'RE 6.42 SECONDS OFF YOUR LAUNCH WINDOW FOR HITTING ALL THE GREEN LIGHTS.

89

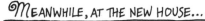

MEANWHILE, AT THE NEW HOUSE...

GOD! ALL OURS! WE CAN PAINT A MURAL! DRIVE SPIKES INTO THE WALLS! PLAY THE PIANO AT MIDNIGHT!

WE DON'T HAVE A PIANO. AND BESIDES, YOU'D WAKE RAFFI. WHERE ARE THOSE **MOVERS**? I BETTER CALL THEM.

MAYBE I'LL GET A DRUM.

SLAM! SLAM!

CLARICE? WHEN DID YOU TELL THE PHONE COMPANY TO START SERVICE HERE?

UM...TOMORROW. IT MADE SENSE AT THE TIME.

WELL, WE CAN'T WAIT AROUND HERE! GO BACK TO THE APARTMENT AND FIND OUT WHAT THE **HELL'S** GOING ON. I'LL STAY IN CASE THEY SHOW UP. I CAN MEASURE FOR BLINDS.

SHIK!

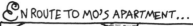

93

I COULDN'T AFFORD A FACTORY-BUILT DINER LIKE THIS WHEN I STARTED OUT. BUILT MY OWN PLACE. I PUT UP A ROOF JUST LIKE YOURS, THOUGH, IN THE SIXTIES, WHEN THE McDONALD'S WENT IN DOWN THE STREET.

YEAH, MY POP ALMOST HAD TO CLOSE DOWN IN 1970, WITH ALL THE FAST-FOOD CHAINS COMING IN. I GUESS PEOPLE LIKE THE PREDICTABILITY. A QUARTER POUNDER'S THE SAME ANYWHERE.

THAT'S FINE IF YOU LIKE THAWED-OUT RETREADS.

THEA? IT'S ME. JUST WANTED TO MAKE SURE YOU AND ANJI HAD EVERYTHING UNDER CONTROL....THE **FIRE EXTINGUISHER?!** BEHIND THE DOOR TO THE OFFICE! WHAT THE **HELL** IS GOING ON?!

CLIK!

NOW WHEN I TRAVEL, I LIKE TO SAMPLE THE LOCAL FARE. YOU FIND SOME **AMAZING** THINGS. HAD A HOT DOG ONCE UP IN OHIO STUFFED WITH CHEESE, WRAPPED IN THICK BACON, AND DEEP FRIED.

WHOA.

HOME COOKING'S A WAY OF LIFE. I WORKED HARD, 13 HOURS A DAY. HAD THREE VACATIONS IN 40 YEARS. ALBERTA'S MOTHER WOULD GET SO MAD AT ME! WE WENT TO FLORIDA ONCE AND I CALLED THE DINER EVERY DAY TO MAKE SURE THEY HADN'T BURNED IT TO THE GROUND.

96

CLARICE! WAIT! WHAT IF HE GOES BACK HOME? ONE OF US SHOULD BE THERE!

DAMN! YOU'RE RIGHT! I'LL GO, YOU KEEP LOOKING?

28TH JOHNSTON

NO, NO. THIS IS ALL MY FAULT. YOU GO, I'LL KEEP LOOKING.

GOOD PLAN!

LISTEN, I DON'T WANT YOU GUYS TO HAVE TO HAUL MY STUFF. I'LL DEAL WITH IT WHEN I GET BACK FROM THE CHIROPRACTOR.

YOU CAN'T EVEN STAND UP!

WE HAVE TO KEEP GOING, STUART. TONI NEEDS THE TRUCK AT TWO. DON'T WORRY, THERE'S NOT THAT MUCH TO MOVE.

I HAVE A FEW BOXES IN THE BASEMENT STORAGE AREA.

GREAT. JUST THE THREE OF US.

LET'S START WITH THE BASEMENT.

A FEW MINUTES LATER...

UH...I'M SURE THEY'LL BE BACK SOON, RAFFI. I BET THEY'RE OUT LOOKING FOR YOU.

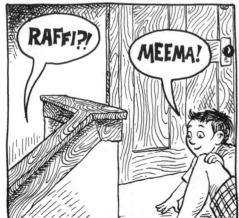

RAFFI?!

MEEMA!

OH, MY LITTLE MONSTER BABY! WHERE HAVE YOU **BEEN?** ARE YOU OKAY? ARE YOU ALL RIGHT**?!**

CAN WE HAVE LUNCH?

MEANWHILE...

...OR PERHAPS STUART ACCRETES THESE MAGAZINES AS A SORT OF BARRIER AROUND HIMSELF, A METAPHORICITY OF THE HETEROMASCULINIST DELUSION OF **IMPENETRABILITY.**

MS. 1975

THE PROGRESSIVE

104

DON'T.

HEY!

I HAVE TO GO.

RAP RAP!

YOU ARE **SUCH** AN ASSHOLE.

LOOK, THIS PETRIFIED MASCULINITY WE'RE ALL **SCHLEPPING** BELONGS TO **YOUR** HOUSEMATE!

UHAUL

IT'S GOING REALLY SLOWLY, GINGER. WE NEED ALL THE HELP WE CAN GET IF WE'RE GONNA MAKE IT TO TONI'S ON TIME.

WHY ARE WE RACING AROUND IN FEAR OF TONI?! SO WHAT IF WE'RE LATE? WHAT'S SHE GONNA DO, **IMPLODE**?

SHE DIDN'T HAVE TO LET US USE THE TRUCK, YOU KNOW. THE LEAST WE CAN DO IS STICK TO HER TIME FRAME. WHAT WERE YOU AND **CLARICE** TALKING ABOUT?

KISS-KISS

SOMETIMES I WONDER IF THERE MIGHT NOT BE SOME VALIDITY TO FREUD'S THEORY OF HOMOSEXUALITY AS ARRESTED DEVELOPMENT.

SMAK SMAK!

SEED

WHERE HAVE YOU **BEEN**?!

TONI, I'M SO SORRY...

THE MOVERS LEFT AN **HOUR** AGO! GOD! I KNOW YOU'RE WRACKED WITH **AMBIVALENCE** BUT CAN YOU **WORK** WITH ME HERE?

I...

WE HAVE TO FINISH PACKING UP THE APARTMENT BEFORE EVERYONE SHOWS UP WITH THE U-HAUL. AND OH, STOP AT THE HARDWARE STORE, WE NEED MORE PACKING TAPE. AND DID YOU...

146 MILES AWAY...

ANJI, WHAT POSSESSED YOU TO TOSS A **CIGARETTE BUTT** IN THE WASTE-PAPER CAN?!

DINER

OPEN 24 HRS

I HAD SOME LOYAL CUSTOMERS! I KNEW HOW THEY LIKED THEIR EGGS. DIDN'T HAVE TO TAKE ANY ORDERS!

AND THERE WAS ALWAYS A CONVERSATION GOING ON! YOU WANTED TO TALK ABOUT WHAT WAS HAPPENING DOWN AT CITY HALL, OR UP IN D.C., OR ACROSS THE STREET, YOU CAME TO AL'S FOR A CUP OF COFFEE. TRY **THAT** AT TACO BELL!

THIS IS TOO MUCH! CARLOS SPILLED THE BEANS!

HE...HE DID?

YEAH, THE EXPENSIVE ORGANIC CANNELLINI ONES. JESUCRISTO! IT'S TWO FIFTEEN! WHERE ARE THOSE PENDEJAS WITH THE TRUCK?

RAFFI! UH...YOU'RE UP!

MOMMY! THE MOVERS CAME AND, UM, I WAS WATCHING, AND THEN, UM, AND THEN I WANTED TO GO SEE THE...

THAT'S NICE, SWEETIE. CLARICE, I'M GOING OVER TO SPARROW'S AND SEE WHAT'S HOLDING THEM UP.

EXCELLENT IDEA, BABE!

SHORTLY...

TONI! HI! UH...WE WOULD'VE CALLED, BUT YOUR PHONE'S DISCONNECTED.

OH MY GOD! ARE YOU JUST GETTING HERE?

WELL, WE HAD SOME UNFORSEEABLE DELAYS.

THERE'S NO TIME FOR DELAYS! I STILL HAVE AN ENTIRE HOUSEHOLD TO MOVE! WHERE IS EVERYONE?!

109

WELL, STUART'S LYING ON THE COUCH. SPARROW WENT OVER TO MY PLACE TO GET AN ICE PACK. GINGER AND LOIS ARE TALKING TO THE ELECTRICIAN, AND SYDNEY WENT TO PEE.

AARGH! DO I HAVE TO DO **EVERY THING**?!

TONI! UM... HI. WE'RE DOING A LITTLE REWIRING. I WAS JUST ASKING LETITIA IF MAYBE WE COULD GET THIS STUFF OUTTA THE WAY, BUT...

I'M RIGHT IN THE MIDDLE OF FISHING THIS WIRE UPSTAIRS. WHAT AM I GONNA DO? PULL IT BACK OUT?

OH, HI, TONI.

SPARROW! D'YOU THINK YOU COULD GET ME A DRINK OF WATER?

HEY! WE'RE ON A **DEADLINE** HERE! HOP TO! LINE UP! SPREAD OUT! WE'RE GONNA FORM A **BUCKET BRIGADE** AND UNLOAD THAT FRIGGING TRUCK!

CLAP CLAP

IMPRESSIVE! HAS SHE DONE PROFESSIONAL DOMINATRIX WORK?

SHE'S JUST UPSET. SHE KNOWS ABOUT CLARICE AND GINGER'S INSANE LITTLE INFATUATION, AND SHE'S, LIKE, DISPLACING ALL HER ANXIETY ONTO GETTING THE U-HAUL BACK ON TIME.

SEEMS TONI FOUND OUT ABOUT CLARICE AND GINGER'S LITTLE **FOLIE À DEUX**. THAT'S WHY SHE'S FIXATED ON THE **TRUCK**.

HA-TCHOO!

Forty-five minutes later...

111

112

113

WELCOME TO THE NEIGHBORHOOD!

I'M ANN. THIS IS BILL, AND BILL JR.

I'M TONI, AND THIS IS CLARICE AND MO AND SPARROW AND GINGER AND SYDNEY AND RAFFI AND LOIS. OH, AND HERE'S CARLOS!

HANG ON, TOTO. I THINK WE'RE IN KANSAS.

ANN, BILL, I DON'T MEAN TO BE RUDE, BUT WE'RE IN A REAL TIME CRUNCH HERE.

SAY NO MORE! I'VE GOTTA GET BACK TO THE GRILL, OR I'D OFFER TO HELP.

WE'LL CHAT LATER.

NICE PEOPLE. THEY LOOK LIKE THEY WERE CONCOCTED BY A FOCUS GROUP.

A DISHWASHER, A MICROWAVE, A WASHING MACHINE WITHOUT COIN SLOTS! IT'S A SLIPPERY SLOPE, BABE. NEXT THING, YOU'LL BE HOSTING A CHAMPAGNE BRUNCH FUNDRAISER FOR THE HUMAN RIGHTS CAMPAIGN! OR **WHATEVER** THE HELL THOSE PEOPLE HOST.

DID SOMEONE SAY **CHAMPAGNE**? SORRY I DIDN'T GET HERE SOONER. LOOKS LIKE YOU'RE ALMOST DONE.

THERE'S STILL PLENTY TO CARRY UPSTAIRS.

OH.

CLARICE, HIT THE LIGHT. IT'S GETTING DARK IN HERE.

FLIP!

115

116

20 MINUTES LATER...

YOU'RE LATE. I WAS JUST ABOUT TO CALL THE POLICE.

GUESS YOU'RE JUST GONNA HAVE TO FINE ME.

SLAP!

WELL, DAD. I HOPE THAT SHOOFLY PIE AT THE MISS ROCHESTER DINER WAS WORTH $300.

WHAT? IT WAS TWO-SEVENTY NINE WITH A DOLLAR TIP! I ALWAYS LIKE TO LEAVE A BIG TIP!

WELL, THAT WORKS OUT FINE, THEN. WE'LL JUST COUNT OUR LOST DEPOSIT AND THE LATE CHARGE AS A BIG OLE TIP FOR U-HAUL!

JEZANNA!

TONI! HEY, THIS WAS THE BIG DAY, WASN'T IT?

THAT'S FOUR-OH-NINE TWENTY.

118

119

SHE ALWAYS WAS MEAN AS CAT SHIT. EXCUSE MY FRENCH, SON.

I CAN'T BELIEVE SHE WOULDN'T WAIVE OUR LATE CHARGES!

IT'S ONLY MONEY.

THERE'S AUDREY WITH THE CAR. DO YOU NEED A RIDE, TONI?

YES! GOD, IN ALL THE CRAZINESS, I FORGOT TO TELL SOMEONE TO PICK US UP! AND YOU CAN BET CLARICE AND THE SIX STOOGES AREN'T GONNA THINK OF IT ON THEIR OWN.

ISN'T THAT CLARICE JUST PULLING IN?

OH.

UH...SO DID YOU GET THE TRUCK BACK ON TIME?

NO. WHEN WERE YOU PLANNING TO TELL ME ABOUT RAFFI'S LITTLE ADVENTURE?

OH. UM... LATER, WHEN YOU WEREN'T SO...SO OVERWROUGHT.

120

I WAS NOT OVER-WROUGHT!

OKAY!

I WAS HYSTERICAL.

THE LIGHTS ARE ON!

YEAH. I CALLED SOMEONE I KNOW AT POWER AND LIGHT. PROMISED HIM I'D LOOK THE OTHER WAY IF HE WANTS TO PUT UP A SUBSTATION NEXT TO AN ORPHANAGE OR SOMETHING.

SO. ARE YOU COMING IN?

I THOUGHT I MIGHT.

WITH THE WAD I'VE GOT INVESTED IN THIS PLACE, I'D BE CRAZY NOT TO.

121

124

Firebrand Books is an award-winning feminist and lesbian publishing house. We are committed to producing quality work in a wide variety of genres by ethnically and racially diverse authors. Now in our fourteenth year, we have over ninety titles in print.

A free catalog is available on request from Firebrand Books, 141 The Commons, Ithaca, New York 14850, 607-272-0000.

Visit our website at www.firebrandbooks.com.